BEST PRACTICES FOR E-Discovery

A Practical Handbook

NICOLE MARIE GILL

ABA
AMERICAN BAR ASSOCIATION
Litigation Section

Cover design by Jill Tedhams/ABA Design

Printed in the United States of America.

29 28 27 26 25   5 4 3 2 1

A catalog record for this book is on file with the Library of Congress.

Discounts are available for books ordered in bulk. Special consideration is given to state bars, CLE programs, and other bar-related organizations. Inquire at Book Publishing, ABA Publishing, American Bar Association, 321 N. Clark Street, Chicago, Illinois 60654-7598.

www.shopABA.org

Contents

Introduction

In today's digital age, the landscape of legal discovery has evolved dramatically. The proliferation of electronic data has transformed the way legal professionals approach the discovery process, making it both a challenge and an opportunity. *Best Practices for E-Discovery: A Practical Handbook* is designed to be an essential guide for practitioners navigating the complexities of e-discovery. This book aims to provide a comprehensive, step-by-step approach to mastering e-discovery, ensuring that legal professionals are well-equipped to handle electronic evidence efficiently and effectively.

The purpose of this handbook is to demystify the e-discovery process and offer practical insights that can be applied in real-world scenarios. Whether you are a seasoned attorney, a paralegal, or a legal IT specialist, this book will serve as a valuable resource, offering best practices, tips, and strategies to streamline your e-discovery efforts. By following the guidance provided in this handbook, practitioners will be able to manage electronic evidence with confidence, reduce risks, and improve outcomes in their cases.

This handbook is structured to walk you through the entire e-discovery process, from initial planning to final production. Each chapter focuses on a specific aspect of e-discovery. Here is a general breakdown of what is covered:

1. **Know the Landscape:** An overview of the rules and regulations that govern the discovery process, helping you understand the legal framework within which e-discovery operates.
2. **Keeping Your Data House in Order:** Guidance on maintaining an organized and efficient data management system to facilitate the e-discovery process.
3. **Initial Considerations:** Key factors to consider at the outset of an e-discovery project, including scope, objectives, and stakeholder involvement.
4. **Identifying the Data:** Best practices for identifying relevant electronically stored information (ESI) that may be subject to discovery.

5. **Preserving the Data:** Techniques for preserving ESI to ensure it remains intact and accessible throughout the discovery process.
6. **Collecting the Data:** Methods for collecting ESI in a defensible manner, ensuring data integrity and chain of custody.
7. **Processing the Data:** Steps for processing ESI to make it reviewable and searchable, including data filtering and de-duplication.
8. **Reviewing and Analyzing the Data:** Strategies for reviewing and analyzing ESI, including the use of technology-assisted review (TAR) and other advanced tools.
9. **Producing and Receiving the Data:** Tips for producing and receiving ESI in a format that is useful and admissible in court.
10. **Sample Documents:** Examples of key documents used in the e-discovery process, providing practical templates and references.

By following the guidance provided in this handbook, you will be able to:

- Develop a solid understanding of the e-discovery process and its importance in modern litigation.
- Create and implement effective e-discovery plans that meet legal and regulatory requirements.
- Identify, preserve, collect, process, review, and produce ESI in a defensible and cost-effective manner.
- Leverage technology to streamline your e-discovery efforts and improve outcomes.

We hope that this handbook will become an indispensable resource for you and your team, helping you navigate the complexities of e-discovery with confidence and success.

Also, a few words of caution: while this resource will help you navigate the e-discovery process, the law and technology in this area is always changing. It is important to pay attention to the changes in laws governing e-discovery in your area and to check back for regular updates to this handbook as we attempt to address large-scale changes in this space.

Chapter 1

Know the Landscape: The Relevant Rules Governing the Discovery Process

I. Introduction

The total amount of digital information in the world is growing exponentially, and according to recent statistics, 402.74 million terabytes of data are created every day.[1] This means that, every year, we are creating approximately 147 zettabytes of data.[2] However, with this astounding and ever-expanding amount of electronic data comes new issues and challenges with digital discovery. Approximately 95 percent of civil litigation matters settle during discovery, and most, if not all, of the evidence at issue in those matters is electronically stored information (ESI). As a result, discovery strategy and management of ESI is a critical success factor in every type of litigation.

Discovery is no longer limited to bankers boxes of paper documents. ESI is now the name of the game. ESI is data or documents created, manipulated, communicated, stored, and best utilized in digital form, requiring the use of computer hardware and software.[3] Electronic discovery (e-discovery) is the exchange of ESI in the course of a legal proceeding. While there is a myriad of ESI sources in today's world, the most common examples include email, servers, social media platforms, cloud-based storage, hard drives, mobile devices, and IoT devices.

To successfully navigate the e-discovery playing field, one must know the relevant rules that drive this discovery, as well as the relevant terminology and technology that underpins electronic discovery. For better or worse, a lawyer must learn to speak tech to be able to properly

1. Troy Beamer, *402.74 Million Terabytes of Data Is Created Every Day*, Tech Bus. News (Oct. 16, 2024), https://www.techbusinessnews.com.au/blog/402-74-million-terrabytes-of-data-is-created-every-day/#:~:text=Reading:%20402.74%20Million%20Terrabytes%20of,staggering%20181%20zettabytes%20by%202025.

2. To put that into perspective, one zettabyte is equal to 1 trillion gigabytes, and just one gigabyte alone holds approximately 64,500 Microsoft Word document pages

3. Kenneth J. Withers, *Electronically Stored Information: The December 2006 Amendments to the Federal Rules of Civil Procedure*, 4 Nw. J. Tech. & Intell. Prop. 171 (2006), https://scholarlycommons.law.northwestern.edu/njtip/vol4/iss2/3.

preserve, identify, collect, review, and produce ESI in the modern world. The ethics rules demand technical competence, and some states are even requiring lawyers to complete technical CLEs.[4] This chapter serves as a roadmap for the remainder of this book, providing a brief overview of the relevant rules governing discovery (i.e., why lawyers need to know about electronic discovery) and a guide to relevant terminology so you can decipher common technical terms.

II. The Rules

A. The Model Rules of Professional Conduct

Putting aside that knowledge of the e-discovery process is necessary for effective representation, the Model Rules of Professional Conduct demand that attorneys know about emerging technologies. In particular, Rule 1.1 Competence states that a "lawyer shall provide competent representation to a client. Competent representation requires the legal knowledge, skill, thoroughness and preparation reasonably necessary for the representation." Comment 8 to this Rule specifically addresses competence, stating that an attorney "should keep abreast of changes in the law and its practice, *including the benefits and risks associated with relevant technology*" (emphasis added).

B. The Rules of Civil Procedure

Both federal and state rules of civil procedure govern the discovery process, and these rules highlight the importance for an attorney to understand the identification, preservation, collection, review, and production of data. In essence, these rules serve as a roadmap for the steps that need to be taken when handling electronic discovery.

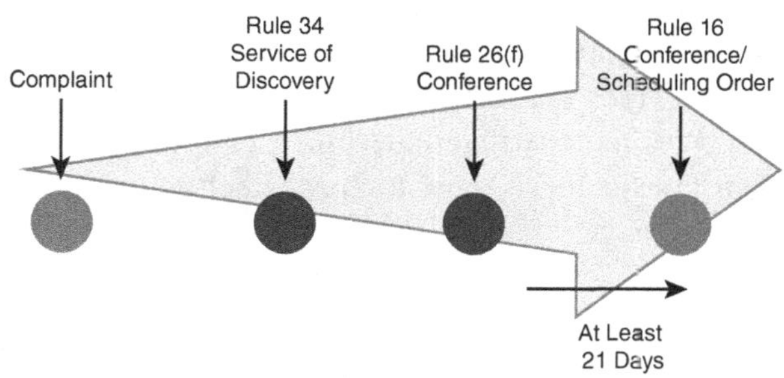

Figure 1.1. How the Federal Rules of Civil Procedure guide discovery from the service of the complaint to the initial conference or scheduling order.

4. For example, Florida requires that at least three credit hours be in technology, and North Carolina requires that at least one credit hour be in technology.

1. Federal Rule of Civil Procedure 1—Attorney Obligation

While Model Rule 1.1 places the onus on the attorney to stay abreast of emerging technologies,[5] the Federal Rules of Civil Procedure also require an attorney to partake in measures to achieve a "just, speedy and inexpensive" outcome for civil litigation.[6] This means both the court and parties should work in a cooperative effort to bring about the main goals of the Rules. This Rule leads the way and demands cooperation and proportionality (see the following section on Federal Rule of Civil Procedure 26) to ensure the just outcome for all parties, including in the realm of discovery.

2. Federal Rule of Civil Procedure 26—Identifying and Collecting Documents

Federal Rule of Civil Procedure 26(b) allows parties to "obtain discovery regarding any nonprivileged matter that is relevant to any party's claim or defense and proportional to the needs of the case, considering the importance of the issues at stake in the action, the amount in controversy, the parties' relative access to relevant information, the parties' resources, the importance of the discovery in resolving the issues, and whether the burden or expense of the proposed discovery outweighs its likely benefit."

While Federal Rule of Civil Procedure 26 allows for broad discovery, there are limitations placed on the discovery of certain ESI. For example, a party need not provide discovery of electronically stored information from sources that the party identifies as not reasonably accessible because of undue burden or cost.[7] (See Chapter 6 for more information pertaining to cost shifting if inaccessible information is sought.) Inaccessible data is generally defined as data that must be restored or reconstructed for production and includes backup tapes and erased or damaged data. (See Chapter 6 for more information pertaining to the production of inaccessible data and the cost-shifting that can accompany it.) Given this broad definition of what is discoverable, along with the reasonable limitations that are placed on the discovery of ESI by the Rules, it is incumbent upon an attorney to understand a client's data prior to an initial meet-and-confer with opposing counsel.

Federal Rule of Civil Procedure 26(f) demands that a conference take place at least 21 days before a scheduling conference is to be held so that parties may confer about a discovery plan. (See Chapter 3 for more information about preparing for a Rule 26(f) Conference.) A discovery

---

5. *See* comment 8 to Model Rule of Professional Conduct 1.1, stating attorneys "should keep abreast of changes in the law and its practice, including the benefits and risks associated with relevant technology."

6. Federal Rule of Civil Procedure 1.

7. Federal Rule of Civil Procedure 26(b)(2)(B).

plan must state the parties' proposals on the subjects on which discovery may be needed, when discovery should be completed, and whether discovery should be conducted in phases or be limited to or focused on particular issues.[8] Any issues about disclosure, discovery, or preservation of electronically stored information as well as issues surrounding claims of privilege or protection of materials should also be addressed at this time.[9]

Rule 26 also requires a party to provide a "a copy—or a description by category and location—of all documents, electronically stored information, and tangible things that the disclosing party has in its possession, custody, or control and may use to support its claims or defenses, unless the use would be solely for impeachment." (See Chapter 4 regarding the identification of data.) It is from the Rule 26(f) conference that a scheduling order will be issued by the judge, providing for the disclosure, discovery, or preservation of electronically stored information, including any agreements the parties reach for asserting claims of privilege or protection.[10]

It is important for attorneys to meaningfully partake in the Rule 26(f) conference to develop a discovery plan and to understand the technology behind their clients' documents. The 2006 Committee Note to the Rule stresses that it may be important for counsel to become familiar with the parties' information systems before a Rule 26(f) conference. For existing clients with repeat litigation, counsel may already have this information at the commencement of litigation. However, for new clients or for litigation involving previously unfamiliar client electronic information systems, outside counsel and in-house attorneys may need to spend significant time with information technology personnel to prepare for the Rule 26(f) meeting in order to converse coherently about the creation and storage of relevant data. Failure to do so could result in sanctions.[11]

3. Federal Rule of Civil Procedure 37—Preserving Documents

Once documents are appropriately identified, the Rules demand that they are appropriately preserved, otherwise sanctions will apply. In particular, Federal Rule of Civil Procedure 37(e) states that if "electronically stored information that should have been preserved in the anticipation or conduct

---

8. Federal Rule of Civil Procedure 26(f)(3).

9. *Id.*

10. Federal Rule of Civil Procedure 16.

11. Federal Rule of Civil Procedure 37(f) ("If a party or its attorney fails to participate in good faith in developing and submitting a proposed discovery plan as required by Rule 26(f), the court may, after giving an opportunity to be heard, require that party or attorney to pay to any other party the reasonable expenses, including attorney's fees, caused by the failure.").

of litigation is lost because a party failed to take reasonable steps to preserve it, and it cannot be restored or replaced through additional discovery, the court" may impose sanctions. The breadth and depth of those sanctions are dictated by how important the data is to the underlying claims, the steps taken (or not taken) to preserve the data, the culpability of the spoliating party, the prejudice to the nonoffending party, the degree of interference with the judicial process, whether sanctions will remedy the harm and deter future spoliation, whether evidence has been irretrievably lost, and the potential for abuse. (See Chapter 5 for more information on spoliation and the sanctions that may result from it.) A court may consider a variety of sanctions in the face of spoliated evidence, including applying the presumption that the lost information was unfavorable to the party, instructing the jury that it may or must presume the information was unfavorable to the party, dismissing the action, or entering a default judgment.[12]

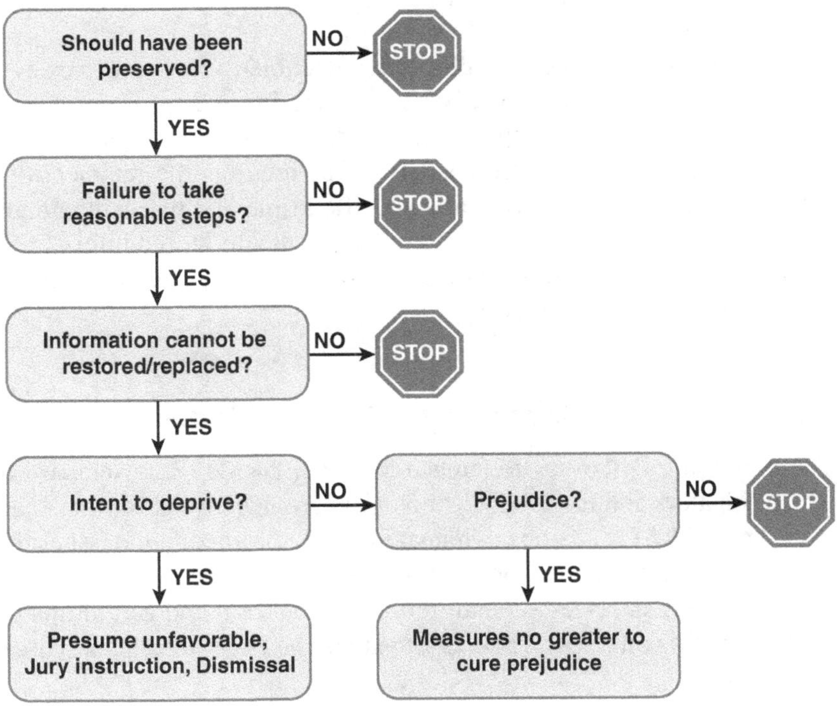

Figure 1.2. How Federal Rule of Civil Procedure 37 is practically implemented in the imposition of sanctions.[13]

12. FEDERAL RULE OF CIVIL PROCEDURE 37(e)(2).

13. PowerPoint Presentation on the Amendments for Education Purposes, LAWYERS FOR CIVIL JUSTICE.

4. Federal Rules of Civil Procedure 34 and 45—Producing Documents

Once a discovery plan is formulated and relevant sources of data are identified, the Rules dictate how documents are to ultimately be exchanged between the parties. Federal Rule of Civil Procedure 34 governs this process. Federal Rule of Civil Procedure 34(a)(1) permits a party to serve on any other party a request "to produce and permit the requesting party or its representative to inspect, copy, test, or sample the following items in the responding party's possession, custody, or control." (See Chapter 3 for information on possession, custody, and control.)

Federal Rule of Civil Procedure 34 also addresses the responses to these requests, stating that a party may object to a request for electronically stored information or to the form of production requested.[14] For data that is produced, documents are "produced as they are kept in the usual course of business or [organized and labeled] to correspond to the categories in the request."[15] (See Chapter 9 for information on the production of data.)

While the exchange of requests for documents between parties is governed by Federal Rule of Civil Procedure 34, Federal Rule of Civil Procedure 45 addresses the production of documents by non-parties. Federal Rule of Civil Procedure 45(a)(1)(A)(iii) requires the recipient of a subpoena "to do the following at a specified time and place: attend and testify; produce designated documents, electronically stored information, or tangible things in that person's possession, custody, or control; or permit the inspection of premises."

III. The Electronic Discovery Reference Model

The Electronic Discovery Reference Model (EDRM) is the standard by which litigators and litigation technologists provide an e-discovery roadmap. The EDRM is an atlas to managing and minimizing the issues that arise when electronically stored information is identified, preserved, collected, processed, reviewed/analyzed, and produced, and can ultimately be described as an attempt to operationalize the Federal Rules discussed earlier.

---

14. Federal Rule of Civil Procedure 34(b)(2).
15. Federal Rule of Civil Procedure 34(b)(2)(E)(i).

A. The History of the EDRM

The EDRM model was first created in 2005 by George Socha Jr. and Tom Gelbmann to "address the lack of standards and guidelines in the eDiscovery industry." Eventually settling on nine stages to address the e-discovery life cycle, Socha and Gelbmann went through three separate versions in 2005 before settling on the 2006 public version. While the overarching themes and categories of these three versions are fundamentally similar, the evolution of these three versions indicates Socha and Gelbmann grappled with how information governance (i.e., records retention) fits into the overall scheme of the EDRM.

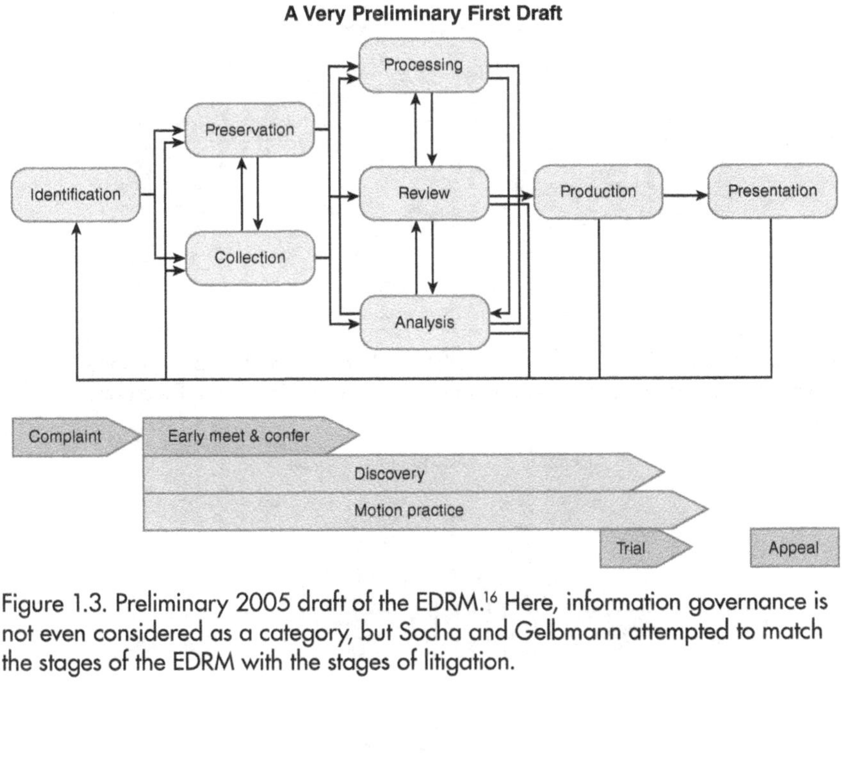

Figure 1.3. Preliminary 2005 draft of the EDRM.[16] Here, information governance is not even considered as a category, but Socha and Gelbmann attempted to match the stages of the EDRM with the stages of litigation.

16. *See EDRM Diagrams—A History*, EDRM (edrm.net), https://edrm.net/resources/frameworks-and-standards/edrm-model/edrm-diagrams-a-history.

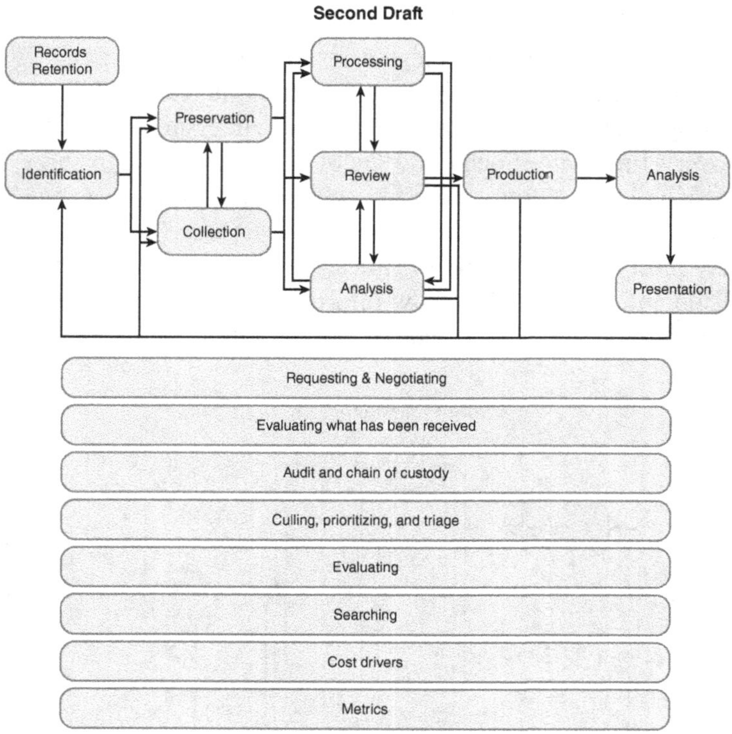

Figure 1.4. Second 2005 draft of the EDRM.[17] Here, information governance is given a place as "records retention," and Socha and Gelbmann list other proportionality considerations.

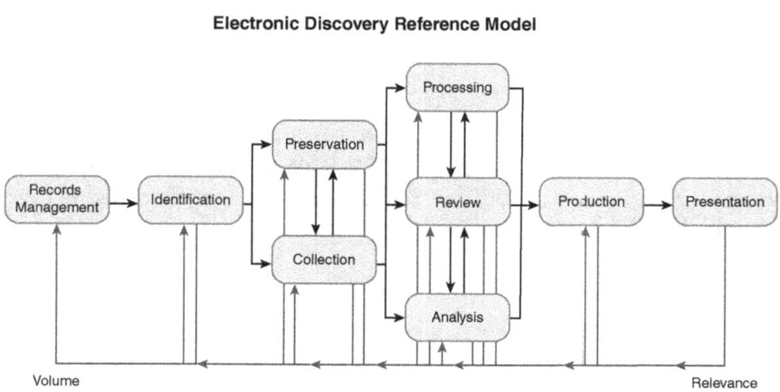

Figure 1.5. Third 2005 draft of the EDRM that was ultimately published for public comment in January 2006.[18] This version laid the rudimentary foundation for the EDRM's nine steps and indicated the importance of proportionality through the consideration of data volume versus relevance.

17. *Id.* at EDRM (edrm.net).
18. *Id.* at EDRM (edrm.net).

With the nine major stages of e-discovery accounted for in the public 2006 version of the EDRM, the 2007 and 2009 versions grappled with identifying the stage that we now know as information governance. First titling it records management and then information management, this slight change to the very first stage of the EDRM indicated that what would later be known as information governance had downstream impact on the life cycle of e-discovery and included more than the management of just records.

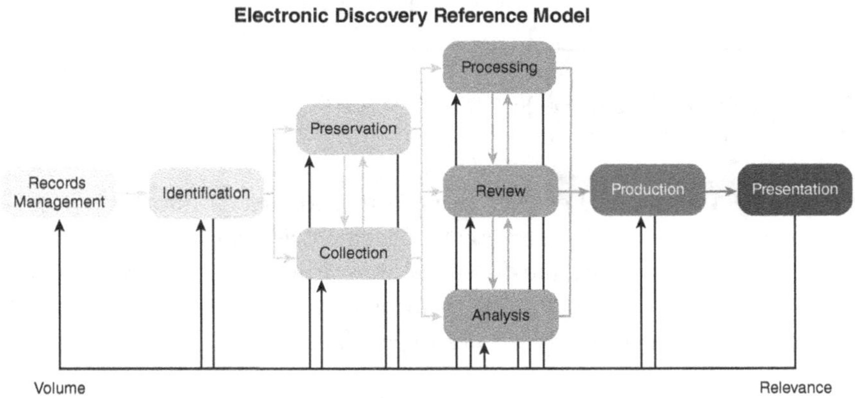

Figure 1.6. The first 2007 version of the EDRM.[19] Note the first stage is identified as records management.

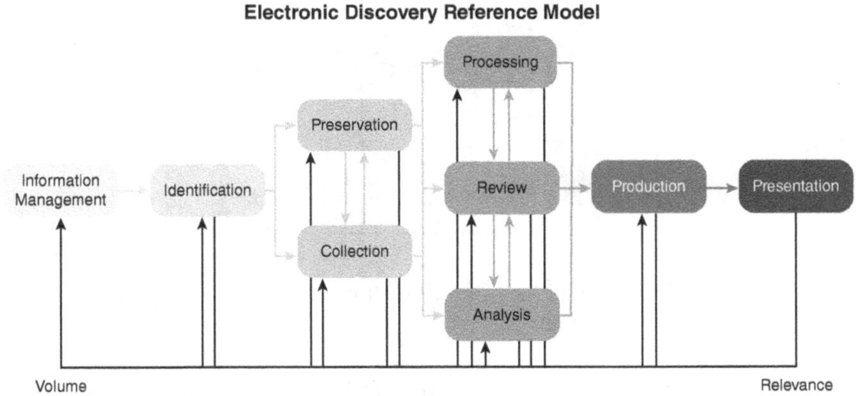

Figure 1.7. The second 2007 version of the EDRM.[20] Note the change in name for the first stage from records management to information management.

19. *Id.* at EDRM (edrm.net).
20. *Id.* at EDRM (edrm.net).

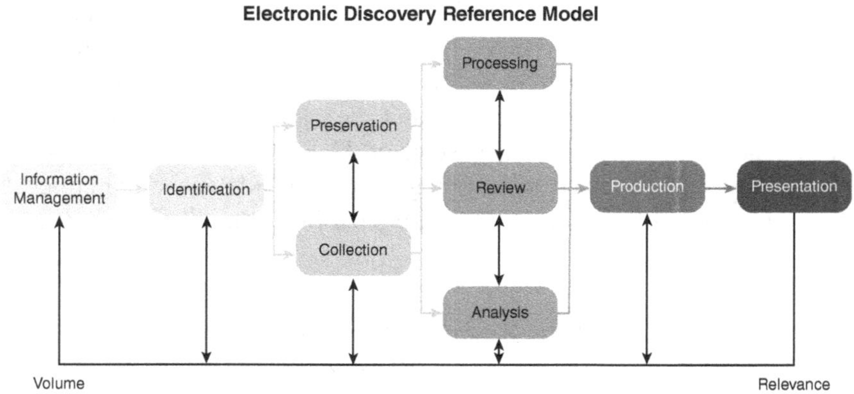

Figure 1.8. The 2009 version of the EDRM.[21] Notice that information management is still the first stage of the model.

By 2014, the model evolved even further to include information governance as opposed to information management as the first stage. While a seemingly minor change, the difference in wording indicates that the overall organization and structure of an institution's data, not just a focus on minor detailed processes, has major impact on the e-discovery life cycle.

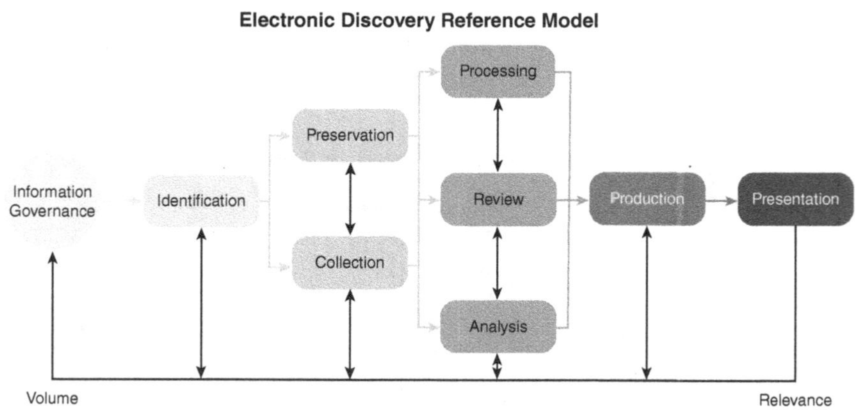

Figure 1.9. The 2014 version of the EDRM.[22] Notice that "information governance" is now the first stage of the model.

There is now a 2023 version of the EDRM that contemplates a standalone Information Governance Reference Model (IGRM) alongside the

21. *Id.* at EDRM (edrm.net).
22. *Id.* at EDRM (edrm.net).

more global EDRM.[23] (See Chapter 2 for more information on information governance and the IGRM.)

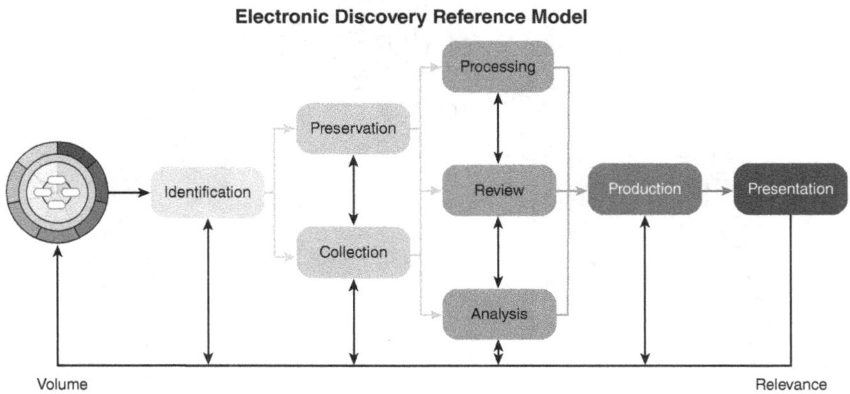

Figure 1.10. The 2023 version of the EDRM that includes the fully fleshed-out IGRM.[24] To see the details contained in the IGRM, see Figure 1.11.

The IGRM offers a model to frame the discussion of information management in the same way the EDRM has shaped the discussion of e-discovery. The diagram focuses on the necessary collaboration amongst key stakeholders when developing information governance policies and procedures. These key stakeholders include business users who need information to operate the organization; IT departments who must implement the mechanics of information management; and legal, risk, and regulatory departments who understand the organization's duty to preserve information beyond its immediate business value.[25] Ultimately, the IGRM highlights the fact that information management is important at all stages of the information life cycle, from its creation through its ultimate disposition.[26]

23. *See Information Governance Reference Model*, https://edrm.net/resources/frameworks-and-standards/information-governance-reference-model.

24. *See Current EDRM Model*, EDRM (edrm.net), https://edrm.net/edrm-model/current.

25. *See Information Governance Reference Model*, EDRM (edrm.net), https://edrm.net/resources/frameworks-and-standards/information-governance-reference-model.

26. *Id.* at EDRM (edrm.net).

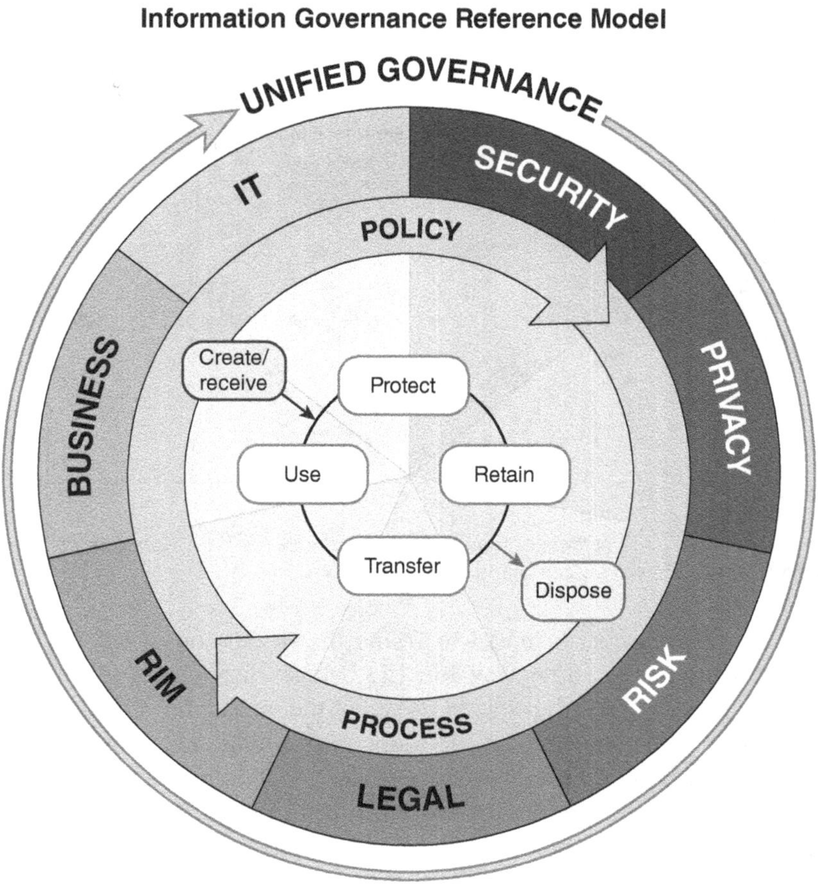

Figure 1.11. The most recent version of the IGRM that shows how various stakeholders need to work together to develop effective information governance policies and procedures.[27]

1. Information Governance

Information governance comprises the policies, processes, and procedures involved in using and managing business information to drive maximum value, while minimizing information-related risk. It applies to all corporate information, regardless of the form, function, or location. It is an iterative program that will involve all parts of the business. Chapter 2 will provide more depth about information governance.

27. *Id.* at EDRM (edrm.net).

2. Identification

Identification involves identifying potential sources of information and utilizing IT and custodial interviews to understand your client's data, who controls it, and where it resides. Chapter 4 will address identification of ESI.

3. Data Preservation

As discussed previously, the preservation of data is an integral part of the discovery process because failure to preserve data can lead to case-changing sanctions. Preservation includes the issuance of litigation holds, knowledge of automatic deletion and overwrite protocols, understanding the impact of employee departures, anticipating other ways in which data commonly disappears, and preventing the deletion or destruction of relevant information in the face of litigation. Chapter 5 covers preservation of data.

4. Data Collection

Collecting data is more than just gathering information on a hard drive; rather, it entails knowing in what form data can—and should—be collected. Chapter 6 provides detail about the collection of relevant data sources.

5. Data Processing

Processing data includes understanding the platforms available to process various data sources. Chapter 7 will provide more depth about processing ESI.

6. Reviewing and Analyzing Data

Reviewing and analyzing data is often the most time-intensive portion of e-discovery. It is at this stage that key documents are identified for use in your case and that essential decisions concerning review strategies are made and employed. Chapter 8 provides strategies for reviewing and analyzing ESI.

7. Producing Data

The form and method of production of data both produced and received is critical, especially when it impacts the review strategy of inbound documents and how documents can be used during trial. Chapter 9 details how to produce relevant ESI.

Chapter 2

Keeping Your Data House in Order

I. Introduction

Long before a complaint is filed, clients are likely to amass an exorbitant amount of ESI. How this data is kept in the ordinary course of business—specifically, how company policies and the basic tenants of information governance are employed—can have positive downstream impacts on discovery. As such, we would be remiss if we did not touch upon the very first, and often overlooked, step in the EDRM: information governance.

II. What Is Information Governance?

As mentioned in Chapter 1, information governance is defined as the policies, processes, and procedures involved in using and managing business information to drive maximum value while minimizing information-related risk. It applies to all corporate information, regardless of the form, function, or location, and addresses the acquisition, storage, access, and ultimate destruction of company data. It is an iterative program that will involve many departments (legal, management, IT, and HR, to name a few) of a business working together to develop appropriate policies to manage and govern electronic data.

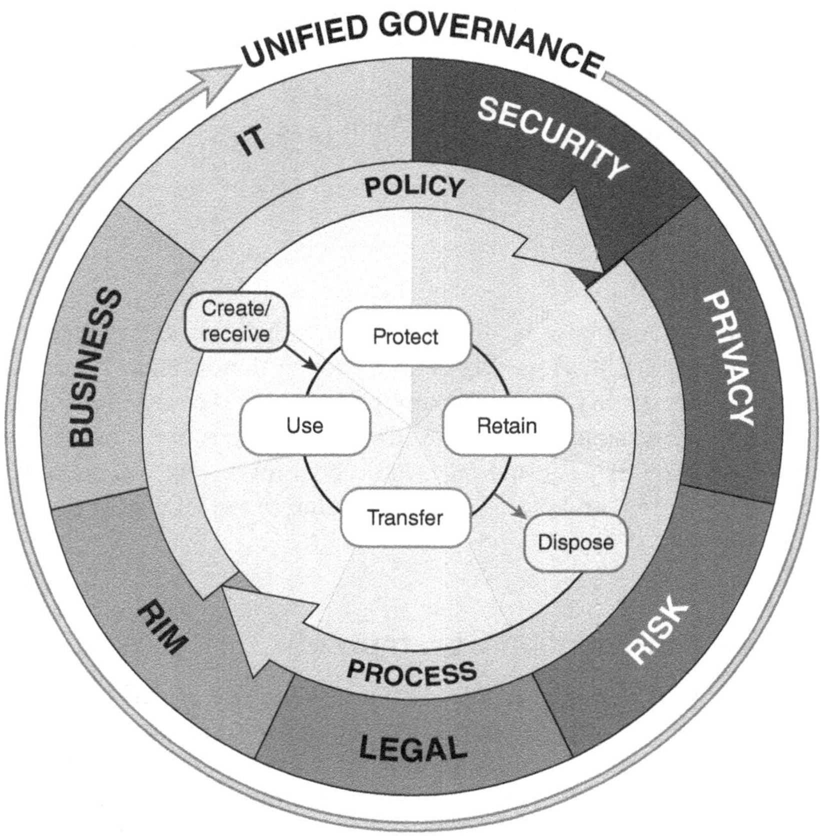

Figure 2.1. The various stakeholders that should ideally be involved in the creation of information governance policies.[1]

III. Goals of Information Governance

The goals of information governance policies are intuitive and can be summarized as follows:

- Control the information life cycle from acquisition or creation to disposal and destruction;
- Prepare, implement, and communicate policies and procedures for information usage;
- Know what information is held, where it is, and in what format;

1. *See Information Governance Reference Model*, EDRM (edrm.net), https://edrm.net/resources/frameworks-and-standards/information-governance-reference-model.

- Know the quality of the information and its exact value to the business;
- Know how the information is stored and what is required to use it;
- Know when the information can be archived and when it can be defensibly deleted;
- Ensure information is available when and where required;
- Ensure information is secure with secure access and confidentiality maintained;
- Equip people within the organization to comply through communication and training;
- Be flexible and able to evolve to meet the changing information formats and communication channels;
- Adhere to the principle of continuous improvement.

IV. Types of Information Governance Policies

A. Relevant Sources of Data

Information governance policies should be uniquely tailored to the company and the types and/or amounts of data a company deals with. Some relevant sources of data to keep in mind when advising your client on the development of information governance policies are:

- **Cloud-based storage.** An internet-based storage platform. Information is essentially housed on the cloud. Examples include Microsoft OneDrive and SharePoint.
- **Email (server based).** Also called a mail server, this is essentially a computer system that sends and receives emails. The information is housed internally. Examples include Amazon SES, Halton MTA, Microsoft Exchange Server, and OpenSMTPD.
- **Email (cloud based).** Cloud-based email is a method of email delivery and storage hosted and maintained by an outside provider. Information is essentially housed on the cloud. Examples include Microsoft Outlook, Yahoo Mail, Google Gmail, and Mozilla Thunderbird.
- **Mobile devices.** Cell phones, including instant and text messaging applications, email applications, and third-party communication applications housed on the phone.
- **Network servers.** A computer program or device that manages network resources and receives and answers requests from clients. This information is essentially housed internally.

- **Social media (Instagram, X (formerly known as Twitter), TikTok).** A tool by which we facilitate the sharing of ideas and information through virtual networks. This category of data is constantly evolving with the development of new social media platforms, and collection methods for the various types of social media will vary. (See Chapter 6 for more on social media collection.)
- **Structured database (on prem and/or cloud).** Typically categorized as quantitative data, structured data is highly organized data that is decipherable by proprietary software. Information for structured databases can be hosted internally on a server or remotely in the cloud. Examples include SQL databases and POS data.
- **Third party collaboration applications (Slack, Microsoft Teams, Google Workspace).** Communication platforms and collaboration hubs that include instant messaging, voice and video calls, and tools to help groups share information and work together.
- **Third-party messaging applications (WhatsApp, Facebook Messenger).** An application other than text messaging that allows individuals to message each other.

B. Types of Governance Policies

Once you have a handle on the types of data your client uses and stores, the next step is to determine which governance policies should be employed to govern that data's life cycle. The following are common information governance policies that are adapted by many businesses to address their data governance needs.

1. Information Security Policies

Information security policies are the rules and guidelines that a company implements to protect its information systems and to keep its data secure. These types of policies ultimately govern security surrounding the access and use of information. Examples of information security policies include the following:

- **Acceptable use policy.** Agreement between a company and its employees expressing an intent to adhere to certain standards regarding usage of company hardware and software.
- **Acceptable encryption and key management policy.** Defines the standards for encrypting and managing sensitive data.

- **Access control policy.** Details requirements that specify how data can be accessed and who can access it.
- **Clean desk policy.** Requires employees to keep their workspaces free of confidential or sensitive information, including client files and folders and external drives that contain sensitive data.
- **Data breach response policy.** Defines procedures for dealing with a data breach within the organization.
- **Disaster recovery plan policy.** Details a company's strategy for handling unplanned events such as natural disasters, cyberattacks, or other data-damaging occurrences.
- **Password policy.** Details the requirements for passwords to access company data, including password length and inclusion of special characters. May also detail how often passwords must be changed and include best practices for keeping passwords safe and secure.
- **Personnel security policy.** Sets standards for hiring, training, and monitoring employees who have access to sensitive data.

2. Records Management Policies

Records management policies focus on a company's procedures for managing its records. These policies address how records are created, stored, accessed, destroyed, or archived. Depending on the type of organization, retention and deletion limits are sometimes prescribed by law, especially when it pertains to a company's retention of personally identifiable information. Please consult local and federal guidelines for your client's particular area of business. Examples of records management policies include the following:

- **Retention and disposal schedules.** Details the types of records held within a company, the minimum period such records should be retained, and the actions taken once that minimum period has been reached.
- **Archiving and deletion policy.** Addresses archiving information (i.e., shifting infrequently accessed data to low-cost storage repositories) and ultimately deleting the data once a minimum retention period has been reached.

3. Remote Working Policies

A policy that has gained more traction in the post-COVID workforce, a remote working policy, or work-from-home policy, is a set of guidelines that outlines how and when it's appropriate for employees to work outside the office. These policies often cover when and how data and other in-office applications may be accessed remotely.

4. Bring Your Own Device Policies

A bring your own device policy (BYOD policy) is a set of rules that governs how employees utilize personal phones, laptops, and other personal devices for work-related purposes. These policies allow employees to access a company's network and applications from their own devices, obviating the need for separate personal and work devices. Note that BYOD policies can have implications on defining possession, custody, and control for purposes of data collection. (See Chapter 4 for more information on possession, custody, and control.)

Chapter 3

Initial Considerations

I. Introduction

As you approach the Rule 26(f) conference, you have hopefully started to consider the depth and breadth of the client data you need to collect. While you may have conducted custodial or IT interviews (see Chapter 4 for more information on these topics), it is possible that you are entering into these initial discovery stages, in particular, the Rule 26(f) conference, without having completed these discovery steps. That is OK. It is important to note that these stages are not hard and fast; rather, they are fluid and will oftentimes overlap or occur at the same time. As such, this chapter begins by addressing the preparation needed for the Rule 26(f) conference regardless of whether you've had time to appropriately interview your IT personnel and/or clients.

II. Hypothetical Case

This section introduces a hypothetical case that will be used throughout the remainder of this book: Polly Plaintiff files suit again Darren Defendant and Corporate Company for wrongful termination. This will walk you through the nuances of each discovery step and exemplify these steps in practice.

Polly Plaintiff v. Darren Defendant and Corporate Company

Polly is a 50-year-old female marketing professional who worked for Corporate Company for 10 years. She worked under her supervisor, Darren, for one year. Polly claims she has a stellar work record and that it was only after Darren became her supervisor that he began to find fault with her work in an effort to edge her out of her position. She claims Darren was attempting to replace her with "fresher" perspectives, i.e., younger talent, even though her work was up to par. She was ultimately placed on a performance improvement plan, and while Polly feels she met the expectations of the plan, Darren disagreed, and Polly was eventually terminated.

Darren is a 35-year-old male who became Polly's supervisor after her previous supervisor retired. As a younger person in this supervisory position, Darren has encouraged his team to develop fresher and innovative ways to meet the needs of their clients, including using various social media outlets. He recently instituted a new department plan that requires his team to utilize these social media outlets and to find new outlets to market Corporate Company's clients. Darren claims Polly has been resistant to these new ideas and that she has stated on many occasions that she refuses to learn the new social media platforms that Darren would like his team to use. It was after Polly's repeated rejection of Darren's plan that Polly was placed on the performance improvement plan and ultimately terminated.

Polly had both a work email account and a personal Gmail account, which she claims she never used for work. She accessed emails from both addresses on her iPhone, which is her own personal device and is governed by a corporate BYOD policy. She claims she texted at least one of her colleagues daily to complain about Darren, and she also claims her work emails will evidence her complaints as well as her stellar work product. She also had a company-issued laptop (a Lenovo ThinkPad) that she promptly returned upon her termination. She utilized Slack to communicate with her colleagues throughout the day. She has personal Instagram and Facebook accounts, though she rarely uses either since both were set up by her colleagues eight years ago. She claims she never used either platform to post about or discuss her employment.

Darren, likewise, has a personal Gmail account as well as a company email account. As a supervisor, he has a work-issued iPhone that only receives work email, and a personal iPhone that only receives his personal email. While he mostly limits using his personal phone and Gmail account for his personal emails and his work phone and work account for his work emails, there may have been times when Darren used his personal email to discuss work with his colleagues. He texts colleagues from both phones because he prefers text messaging over Slack. Darren also has a work-issued laptop (a Lenovo ThinkPad). While Darren has personal TikTok and SnapChat accounts, he never uses them to discuss work.

Corporate Company is a corporation that issues laptops to all its employees. When an employee leaves, company policy dictates that the individual's emails are archived and stored for one year along with any documents the employee may have saved to her desktop. Once this data is archived, the laptop is then wiped and repurposed for another user. The company also utilizes an Enterprise Outlook account to manage its company email and utilizes a network Sharepoint site for employees to save documents that can be seen and worked on collaboratively. As mentioned previously, it has a BYOD policy for employees without a company-issued cell phone, and it gives company-issued iPhones to supervisors. Those individuals who have a company-issued iPhone do not receive the BYOD policy; rather, it is company policy that supervisors only use the company iPhone to conduct business. The company also started to utilize Slack a few years ago under a business license, and employees regularly utilize this messaging application to communicate with each other throughout the workday.

III. Preparing for a Rule 26(f) Conference

As mentioned in Chapter 1, Federal Rule of Civil Procedure 26(f) demands that a conference take place at least 21 days before a scheduling conference and requires that the parties consider the nature and basis of their claims and defenses and the possibilities for promptly settling or resolving the case, make or arrange for the disclosures required by Rule 26(a)(1), discuss any issues about preserving discoverable information, and ***develop a proposed discovery plan*** (emphasis added). This discovery plan must state the parties' proposals on the subjects on which discovery may be needed, when discovery should be completed, and whether discovery should be conducted in phases or be limited to or focused on particular issues.

When preparing for the Rule 26(f) conference, here are a few practice pointers to consider:[1]

1. **Know your case.** The more informed you are about the facts and issues of your case, the more capable you will be at identifying potential sources and topics of relevant information, comprehending the amount of data you may have to review and the time implications this may have on discovery, and understanding potential privilege or preservation issues.
2. **Talk to your client.** While it is ideal to conduct both IT and client interviews prior to the Rule 26(f) conference (see Chapter 4 for more information on these topics), at the very least, have a conversation with your client to discuss the potential sources of data that exist and who may be in possession of that data.

1. Adapted from Ebony S. Morris, *Four Tips for Productive Rule 26(f) Conferences*, Am. Bar Association (Dec. 31, 2019), https://www.americanbar.org/groups/litigation/committees/pretrial-practice-discovery/practice/2019/four-tips-for-productive-rule-26f-conferences.

3. **Work with opposing counsel.** Use this time with opposing counsel to conduct a meaningful conference that contemplates and sets a path toward resolution of potential discovery issues.
4. **Recap.** After the conference, write to opposing counsel, memorializing the points of agreement, points of disagreement, and action items, scheduling a follow-up meet-and-confer if needed.

A sample Rule 26(f) memorandum as presented by the Eastern District of Pennsylvania can be found in the appendix.

IV. ESI Protocol Basics

What is ultimately born out of a collaboration between counsel that starts with the Rule 26(f) conference is an ESI Protocol. An ESI Protocol is a negotiated document that expressly states how the parties to a litigation should produce ESI, and ideally, this will be drafted and negotiated once the attorney has more information on the amount, types, and location of her client's data (see Chapter 4 for more information on identifying data).

While not necessary, the ESI Protocol can be submitted to the court as a stipulation and order. There are benefits and drawbacks to having a court enter an order governing ESI. On the one hand, a court order will ensure that the parties adhere to the agreements reached regarding electronic discovery. However, discovery is a fluid process. While you may begin the electronic discovery process thinking you have a finite data set, further interviews may reveal a much larger data set. Because electronic discovery can be unpredictable in this way, it is advisable that an ESI protocol evolve and that discussions regarding ESI remain iterative. In this regard, it is often cumbersome and time-consuming to have to petition the court for changes to an entered order every time another unforeseen circumstance arises with electronic discovery.

Ultimately, the goals of an ESI protocol are:

- to define a process that the parties agree on for identifying the scope of relevant data to be preserved and produced;
- to identify the form of production for different types of data, what fields of metadata will be produced, and to determine a process for reviewing native data, if provided;
- to outline the process for creating and challenging the privilege log, and;
- to define how the parties will treat inadvertently produced privileged material. A FRE 502(d) order may accompany the ESI protocol, or clawback provisions may be incorporated into it to address inadvertently produced privileged material. Additionally,

parties should incorporate or enter separately a confidentiality order to protect their clients' data.

Don't worry if any or all the terms utilized above seem to be written in a foreign language. What follows is a breakdown of each of these goals, defining any technical terms in the process. While the component parts of each of these goals are more substantively addressed in the following chapters, at least a preliminary knowledge of this information will help kickstart your ESI protocol negotiations.

A. Identifying the Scope of Relevant Data to Be Preserved and Ultimately Produced

While the best means of accessing the scope of data to be preserved is gleaned through interviews with your client and client's IT (see Chapter 4 for more information regarding these interviews), consider these initial questions when identifying data early on:

1. Who Is Likely to Have Relevant Information?

Consider parties, non-parties, and potential expert witnesses.

In Polly's lawsuit, the obvious individuals with relevant information are Polly and Darren. But what about the individuals Polly texted on a daily basis or the colleagues Darren may have talked to about Polly? How can these individuals be identified? Who else made key HR decisions related to Polly's previous reviews and termination? Will a corporate designee be needed for Corporate Company?

2. What Are My Likely Sources of Information?

Consider all relevant sources of information, from email and text messages to social media platforms and third-party messaging applications.

In Polly's lawsuit, Polly's work emails would be important as well as Darren's and the emails of any individuals involved in Polly's ultimate termination. Darren's personal emails may also be relevant along with his text messages from his two cell phones. Polly also seems to have relevant text and Slack messages. There are likely HR files that may be housed on the SharePoint site that are also relevant.

3. How Much Information Is Expected?

Depending on the number of custodians, the relevant time period, and the number of sources of information, the amount of data expected will dictate how you negotiate specific ESI protocol terms (more on this ahead).

In Polly's lawsuit, there is likely a significant amount of email as well as HR files that will be pulled because Polly worked for the company for 10 years. There are methods that can be used to cull that large data set down (this will be discussed more in Chapter 8), but for now, this is something to consider early on when agreeing to certain ESI protocol terms. Additionally, Darren's two email addresses are relevant for a one-year period, as well as Polly's Slack messages for at least a two-year period and Polly's text messages for at least a one-year period.

B. Identifying Form of Production, Metadata, and Natives

The format of production is covered in Chapter 9, but some initial questions to consider when initially developing your ESI protocol are:

1. **What metadata do I have, and what metadata am I willing to produce?** Metadata is a set of data that describes and gives information about other data. For example, an email often contains metadata fields that correspond with who sent the email, who received the email, the subject of the email, and the time and date on which it was sent. While metadata is discussed more fully in Chapter 7, consider the implications of providing certain metadata fields to opposing counsel as well as the onus of fulfilling the obligation to produce those fields.
2. **In what form am I producing and receiving data?** Reviewing documents in a review platform may necessitate the need for one form of production, while reviewing standard PDFs will require a different form of production. Again, while the form of production is discussed more fully in Chapter 9, this is something that should be contemplated at the ESI protocol stage.

C. Creating a Privilege Log

Depending on the amount of data you will be producing, certain privilege logs may be more suitable to your case because of time constraints. Consider whether a metadata log, a categorical log, or a standard privilege log is most suitable for the amount of data you will be withholding. (See Chapter 8 for more information on the types of logs and the benefits and drawbacks of each.)

D. Inadvertent Disclosures and Rule 502(d) Orders

Despite a reviewer's most diligent efforts, human error can lead to the inadvertent disclosure of privileged information. Exactly how an attorney can claw back inadvertently disclosed privileged information is prescribed by Federal Rule of Evidence 502. In particular, FRE 502 states that, in a federal proceeding, the production of an attorney-client communication or work product protected document does not constitute a waiver if:

- the disclosure is inadvertent;
- the holder of the privilege or protection took reasonable steps to prevent disclosure;
- and the holder promptly took reasonable steps to rectify the error,[2] including (if applicable) following Federal Rule of Civil Procedure 26(b)(5)(B).[3]

FRE 502 permits a federal court to enter an order stating that production of documents protected by the attorney-client privilege or work product doctrine does not waive those protections in the specific litigation or any other federal or state proceeding. This is known as a 502(d) order and can be part of the initial negotiations between counsel when discussing discovery obligations. These orders typically include the notification requirements for the producing party as well as the steps the receiving party may take to challenge the clawback.

This fail-safe is one that should be genuinely considered before considerable documents are exchanged. In fact, the Honorable Andrew Peck (retired) has said, "For anyone likely to produce more than a handful of documents, it would be akin to malpractice to not seek a 502(d) nonwaiver order in federal court."[4]

A sample 502(d) order as printed from the Sedona Conference's Commentary on Protection of Privileged ESI can be found in the appendix.

E. Confidentiality Agreements

In addition to 502(d) orders, the parties may agree among themselves to limit disclosure of discovery information to certain specified persons during the litigation. Court approval of such an agreement or a court order is not necessary, but like the ESI protocol itself, an order can be entered.

---

2. In the infamous case of Alex Jones whereby the Infowars host was sued by the parents of the victims of the Sandy Hook shooting, Alex Jones's counsel mistakenly sent a digital copy of Jones's entire cell phone to opposing counsel. When informed by opposing counsel of the error, Jones's counsel still did not take any steps to identify it as privileged or protect it in any way. As such, the inadvertent disclosure constituted a waiver of the privilege, and Jones's attorney eventually had his law license suspended because he "failed to provide even the minimal amount of attention and care required when it came to handling the plaintiffs' sensitive discovery materials." *Lafferty v. Jones*, No. X06UWYCV186046436S, 2023 WL 153608 (Conn. Super. Ct. Jan. 5, 2023), error dismissed in part, 220 Conn. App. 724 (2023).

3. Federal Rule of Evidence 502(b).

4. Cristin Taylor, *What Is a 502(d) Order and Why Should You Care?*, Relativity Blog (June 30, 2021), https://www.relativity.com/blog/what-is-a-502-d-order-and-why-should-you-care.

Confidentiality agreements are most appropriate in litigation where the disclosure of confidential information could reveal sensitive personal or business information. In these instances, information is typically categorized into several categories of confidentiality: confidential, highly confidential, and/or attorneys' eyes only. The application of each of these designations depends on the sensitivity of the information being disclosed, and the order itself typically contains the following: (1) definitions of what constitute confidential and highly confidential/attorneys' eyes only information, (2) procedures for challenging a confidentiality designation, (3) steps to correct an inadvertent failure to designate a document's confidentiality, (4) methods for use of confidential information, and (5) remedies for disclosure of confidential information.

A sample Model Confidentiality Stipulation and Proposed Protective Order from the United States District Court for the Southern District of New York and a sample Model Confidentiality Order from the United Stated District Court for the Northern District of Illinois can be found in the appendix.

V. Detailed Information about ESI Protocols

While ESI protocols are as unique as the cases they support, there are standard categories that an attorney should consider incorporating into her protocol. The easiest way to walk through this exercise is to present you with a very comprehensive ESI protocol and then to explain each section one by one so that you understand the nuances. While each of these categories are only briefly covered here for purposes of the ESI protocol, they will be covered in more depth in later chapters so that you can have a comprehensive understanding of what each of these terms means and these steps entail. For now, consult the Order Regarding Production of Electronically Stored Information and Paper Documents (ESI Protocol) in the appendix to view each section referred to below.

A. General Provisions

The general provisions section of an ESI protocol typically lays out the standard terms of the agreement, including to whom it applies, important deadlines governing the protocol, definitions for key terms in the protocol, whether a confidentiality agreement has been entered in the matter, and an agreement on encryption and the security of data. These terms can be edited, added, or deleted depending on the needs of your case.

B. General Production Format Protocols

The section detailing general production format is where technology truly meets e-discovery. This section details the form of production (also discussed in Chapter 9), including details on Bates numbering and confidentiality branding as well as treatment of document families.

1. Forms of Production

Let's first look at sections II.A.–II.C. of the sample ESI Protocol in the appendix. These sections provide information pertaining to the production of various types of documents. In particular, sections A, B, and C of the sample contemplate the production of unstructured data as well as Excel spreadsheets, personal databases, and audio/visual files. Unstructured data is information that is not arranged according to a preset data model, and therefore cannot be stored in a traditional database. Email is an example.

This protocol also contemplates the use of optical character recognition or OCR (see section II.B.1. of the sample ESI Protocol). OCR is sometimes referred to as text recognition, and an OCR program extracts and repurposes data from scanned documents, camera images, and image-only PDFs. OCR software singles out letters on the image, puts them into words, and then puts the words into sentences, thus enabling access to and editing of the original content. It also eliminates the need for manual data entry and makes documents such as PDFs searchable.[5]

Other file types, such as Excel or audio/visual files, do not often ingest well into a review platform. As such, section C contemplates the production of these types of files in their native, original, format so that they can be viewed accordingly.

The paragraphs on forms of production also refer to how the data is going to be produced to the opposing party (more on this distinction in Chapter 9). When using a review platform, the most common method of receiving unstructured data is TIFFs with Text files. While these acronyms and words may seem confusing, they merely state that data will be produced with TIFF images and text files so that they can be appropriately ingested and viewed within review software. (See Chapter 7 for more information on available review software.)

5. *What Is OCR (Optical Character Recognition)?*, https://aws.amazon.com/what-is/ocr.

2. Bates Numbering

Section II.E. of the sample ESI Protocol addresses Bates numbering (also known as Bates stamping, Bates branding, Bates coding, or Bates labeling). Bates numbering is a method of sequentially numbering pages with a reference number. While traditionally done with a stamp by hand, modern technology allows for easy Bates stamping within a review platform.

Typically, each page is branded with a unique identifying number that often begins with several letters from the party's name, such as ABC-CORP_000001. It is important to note that native documents (such as videos and photos) cannot be branded. As such, if a document is produced natively, a single slipsheet image is put in the place where the native was produced, and that slipsheet bears the Bates stamp.

3. Treatment of Families

Documents sometimes are singular, but often they come as a family. A document family is made of the main document (the parent) and that document's attachments (the children). For example, for an email attaching two documents, the email itself is the parent and the attachments are the children.

It is important to maintain the family relationships of documents because producing a document without its family context can often be misleading. As such, ESI protocols often address the family relationship within production and contemplate the production of families together, as you will see in section II.F. of the sample ESI Protocol. As this sample shows, and what is standard practice, if a main document is responsive and the attachments are nonresponsive, the entire document family is often produced. Similarly, if a main document is responsive and one of its attachments is privileged, the main document will typically be produced while the privileged attachment will be redacted in full or replaced with a slipsheet. (See Chapter 8 for more information on privilege review.)

4. Production Specs and Metadata

Sections II.H. and II.G. of the sample ESI Protocol address production specifications. When specifying the particulars of a production and utilizing a review platform, it is best to ask for a load file with corresponding metadata. A load file will connect the metadata received to each document so that you will be able to see, for example, when a document has been created, last viewed, or even last modified. (See Chapter 7 for the most common metadata fields exchanged during discovery.)

These provisions also contemplate whether productions should be made in color or black and white. (See section II.I. of the sample ESI

Protocol.) While a seemingly small decision, the production of color images can be more expensive since the general size of color documents is larger; however, the inclusion of color may be necessary for document clarity (i.e., presenting various colored highlights in a document).

Finally, section II.K. specifies how data should be transmitted. The most common methods for document transfer are encrypted hard drives, flash drives, or secure file transfer protocols (SFTPs). Oftentimes, the size of the data being transmitted dictates how a transfer will occur, as exceedingly large productions can sometimes be difficult through an SFTP. Regardless of the method chosen, it is imperative that the transfer of data occur in a secure environment. For more information on the appropriate means to transfer data, consult Chapter 9.

5. Confidentiality Designations

Section II.J. of the sample ESI Protocol addresses confidentiality. This paragraph should be edited to reflect any confidentiality or protective order entered into for your matter and branding (the stamping of confidential, highly confidential, or whichever agreed-upon confidentiality terms have been decided) should be edited to reflect the same. For more information on these types of orders and agreements, consult the section on confidentiality agreements in this chapter.

C. Paper Document Production

While this book deals with electronic discovery, concessions still need to be made for paper documents that a client or opposing party may have and that may need to be produced. In this digital world, even paper documents are now digitized for purposes of production, which ultimately makes transfer more secure and review much easier. Section III of the sample ESI Protocol accounts for this.

Paper documents are typically scanned into a digital form, using either a vendor or personal office scanner, to create a resultant PDF file.[6] Once these files are scanned, OCR is used to make these documents text searchable (see previous section for a discussion of OCR).

Paper documents are also typically unitized. Unitization is the process of packaging documents into their logical families. For example, if your client has a file folder, and inside that folder he has seven multi-paged documents, each multi-paged document would be scanned to create seven separate documents as opposed to each page being its own

6. See Chapter 9 for more information on what a PDF file is as well as other file formats that are used for production.

separate document or, even worse, having all of the documents scanned together as one document. Unitization also considers keeping file and binder structures intact so that when documents are digitized, the resultant file structure you see on the screen is reflective of what exists in hard copy. For the example above, the resultant scans would show a digital file folder containing seven digital files.

D. ESI Metadata Format and Processing

Sections IV.B. and IV.C. of the sample ESI Protocol also considers the metadata fields to be produced between the parties, memorializing the agreed upon time zones and addressing whether metadata fields can be redacted in the face of certain privilege. (See section H for more information on addressing privilege in the ESI protocol as well as Chapter 8, which addresses privilege and redactions.) A more robust explanation of metadata fields is covered in Chapter 7.

E. Paring the Review Down

The obvious goal of a document review in general is to pare down the document realm as much as possible so that the truly relevant information can be reviewed in an efficient and cost-effective matter. To that end, there are several terms within an ESI protocol that are incorporated with the goal of reducing the volume of irrelevant documents that are produced.

1. De-NISTing

Section IV.A. of the sample ESI Protocol mentions de-NISTing[7] during processing. De-NISTing is a method of reducing the number of documents subject to review by removing file types that are unlikely to be responsive or have evidentiary value. Examples of file types removed during de-NISTing are files used to execute computer programs, help files, and font files. Many e-discovery review platforms offer the ability to de-NIST, and application of this process is commonplace.

7. NIST stands for the National Institute of Standards and Technology. This agency maintains a list that is updated four times a year and is part of the National Software Reference Library Project. When software is used to de-NIST, the software compares all ESI in a collection against the National Software Reference Library list and removes files matching those on the list unlikely to contain relevant information. *See What Does DeNIST Mean and Why Should You Care?*, PERCIPIENT, https://percipient.co/denist-mean-care.

2. Email Threading

Section IV.D. allows emails to be threaded. An email thread is a series of related emails that are organized and linked together to form a conversation. The first message is usually at the bottom, while the most recent message is seen first at the top. For example, if Amy Attorney emails Carl Client and Carl Client emails Amy Attorney back, Amy's first email to Carl will appear at the bottom of the page and Carl's latest email will appear at the top, with all back-and-forth correspondence appearing on one document. By allowing email threading, only the most inclusive thread of an email will be produced, which obviates the need to re-read lesser inclusive threads (i.e., Amy Attorney's initial email to Carl Client) with duplicative information.

3. De-duplication

Section IV.E. of the sample ESI Protocol allows for de-duplication. Essentially, any document that occurs multiple times within a group of documents will only be produced once; however, all individuals who had that document in their possession would be accounted for in the metadata. For example, if Amy Attorney and Carl Client both have the same email in their inboxes, de-duplication efforts would produce this email only one time; however, the metadata exchanged would show that both Amy and Carl had copies of this email in their respective mailboxes.

4. Zero-Byte Files

Section IV.F. allows for the withholding of zero-byte files, or those files that do not contain any sizeable or meaningful data.

F. Other Document Factors to Consider

Electronic documents have their own quirks, and while every single one of them cannot be accounted for in the ESI protocol, there are a few that are continually addressed because of their common place fixture in e-discovery, as in sections IV.G. to IV.K. of the sample ESI Protocol.

1. Microsoft Auto Feature

A host of Microsoft products, including Word and Excel, allow for auto fields to populate every time the document is opened. For example, a date can be added to a memo so that every time the document is edited, the newest date is automatically populated. This auto population can be deceiving, as it could, in the example, give an incorrect date for when the document was created. This feature is accounted for by producing documents with an auto style field (i.e., auto date where the date is in the example), so the receiving party does not receive misleading information. This feature is something that can be automatically accounted for in a review platform.

2. Hidden Text

Some documents, especially Microsoft Excel spreadsheets and PowerPoints, can have hidden columns or hidden text. To the extent hidden content exists, documents are often produced with that hidden material. It is also important to be aware that hidden data may exist in the documents you are reviewing and ultimately producing. Be sure to review this hidden data to make sure it is not privileged or highly sensitive.

3. Embedded Objects

PowerPoints and Word documents often have images or tables embedded into the document. Produced documents often extract these embedded objects and save them as separate documents, so that if a document is produced, any embedded object is also produced as its own document. In the case of an Excel spreadsheet with an embedded table, for example, the spreadsheet would be produced as one document and the embedded table would be separated out as its own document.

4. Compressed Files

The most common type of compressed file is a zip file. A zip file is a computer file whose contents of one or more files are compressed for storage or transmission. Essentially, zip files take large files and compress their contents so they take up less space. Because zip files are not recognizable by most review platforms, documents are produced unzipped so they can be appropriately processed.

5. Password Protected Documents

It is customary to make a good-faith effort to unlock any password protected documents by consulting with your client to obtain the passwords. However, should you not be able to find the password for a particular document, there is software available that can essentially break open an otherwise password protected document. This provision accounts for the existence of password protected documents and the possible use of password-cracking software.

G. Use of Search Terms and Other Review Methodologies

As mentioned previously, one goal of e-discovery is to whittle down the document realm into a manageable set for review and use for a matter.

Section V of the sample ESI Protocol accounts for the use of several methods a producing party can employ to appropriately cull down a document review set.

The most important part of this section refers to the meet and confer of this iterative process since the agreement of both parties on discovery issues will meaningfully drive the discovery process forward. Of course, the application of date parameters, search terms, custodians (a fancy, technical term for owner of the information), and other review modalities (such as technology-assisted review) certainly need to be discussed and agreed upon by the parties. Again, this is a cursory overview for sake of the protocol, but a more robust discussion of review and analysis of documents can be found in Chapter 8.

Provisions also are made for the review of structured data. Structured data is often only viewable in proprietary software and databases, so the most effective methods for enabling the receiving party to review this material should be discussed. Oftentimes, this data is queried by the producing party so that only relevant information is received by the requesting party in a meaningful (i.e., spreadsheet) format. Other times, parties can agree to give requesting parties limited or supervised access to databases to conduct a limited search.

Lastly, the production of cell phone data and social media data, to the extent it is relevant, is accounted for. (See Chapter 6 for more information on the collection methods for these types of data.) Particularly for text messages, along with messaging application data such as Teams and Slack, it is important to consider the form of production as well as the time-period that constitutes a "message." Since a message string could go on for days, weeks, or even months, and seemingly extend outside the relevant time period or even the relevant subject matter, explicitly stating what time period should be produced on either side of a relevant message is important. The most common time period utilized is 24 hours. (See Chapter 9 for more information on the production of this type of data.)

H. Privilege and Redactions

Section VI of the sample ESI Protocol details the type of privilege log the parties are agreeing to (see Chapter 8 for the different types of privilege logs and the advantages and drawbacks of each) as well as the types of documents that do not need to be logged. For example, so long as the reason for a redaction is apparent on its face (i.e., the redaction says either "attorney client communication" or "attorney work product") and the relevant metadata is viewable, it is most efficient to not include redacted documents on a privilege log. This section also addresses the procedures for challenging a claim of privilege.

I. Clawbacks

Section VII of the sample ESI Protocol discusses the procedure for asserting a clawback and the process for which the challenge will be heard by the court. For more on clawbacks, see the previous discussion on Inadvertent Disclosures.

J. Miscellaneous

Lastly, an ESI protocol often contains some standard language that addresses miscellaneous provisions preserving the rights and objections of all parties. In particular, section VIII of the sample ESI Protocol details the procedure for the production of otherwise inaccessible ESI and the potential shifting of costs for having to obtain and produce such discovery. (See Chapter 6 for more on the procedures for cost-shifting for otherwise unobtainable ESI.)

Chapter 4

Identifying the Data

I. Introduction

This chapter will discuss how to identify potential sources of information, including utilizing IT and custodial interviews to understand your client's data, who controls it, and where it resides.

II. Potential Sources of Information

Before you begin interviewing potential custodians, you first need to understand who may have relevant information (i.e., who do you need to interview) and what sources of information are available.

A. Custodians

In determining who the relevant custodians, or keepers, of information are, it is best to have a conversation with your client. It is from this conversation that you will learn who the key players are in the matter and thus who is likely to have information that is relevant and discoverable. Note that while you may cast your initial net wide with a very long list of custodians, and while you may eventually collect data from all these custodians, that does not necessarily mean that you will review and produce data from all of these custodians. The decision of which custodial data you will eventually search, review, and produce is an iterative process that is undertaken by meet and confers with opposing counsel and that considers balancing the cost of discovery with the amount in controversy. Early meetings with opposing counsel often lead to an initial list of custodians to be searched, with both sides reserving the right to ask for additional custodians to be searched if the first round of discovery shows that other custodians had a significant role. For example, if Peter and Paul are on the initial list, and a review of their documents shows that there are many relevant emails exchanged with Mary, someone would (and could) ask for Mary's emails to be gathered and produced at a later date.

In Polly's lawsuit, Polly and Darren are obvious custodians, but an interview with Polly will reveal which colleague she texted daily to complain about Darren. The name of this individual is important, as this individual is a custodian with relevant information, and that information needs to be preserved and collected. Additionally, interviews with Darren and a representative from Corporate Company will reveal key decision makers who ultimately were integral in Polly's termination. These custodians will likely have relevant information that needs to be preserved and collected.

B. Sources of Data

As was discussed in Chapter 2, the most common sources of electronic data are listed below. Keep these data types in mind when conducting your custodial interviews but be sure to be thorough in your questioning by continually asking about other software or data types; storage devices, including everything from old floppy disks to boxes of hard copy documents; and storage locations, including backups and archived data, that may not be mentioned below, including proprietary software.

- **Cloud-based storage.** An internet-based storage platform. Information is essentially housed in the cloud. Examples include Microsoft OneDrive and SharePoint.
- **Email (server based).** Also called a mail server, this is essentially a computer system that sends and receives emails. The information is essentially housed internally. Examples include Amazon SES, Halton MTA, Microsoft Exchange Server, and OpenSMTPD.
- **Email (cloud based).** Cloud-based email is a method of email delivery and storage hosted and maintained by an outside provider. Information is essentially housed in the cloud. Examples include Microsoft Outlook, Yahoo Mail, Google Gmail, and Mozilla Thunderbird.
- **Mobile devices.** Cell phones, including instant and text messaging applications, email applications, and third-party communication applications.
- **Network servers.** A computer program or device that manages network resources and receives and answers requests from clients. The information is essentially housed internally.
- **Social media (Instagram, X (formerly known as Twitter), TikTok).** A tool by which we facilitate the sharing of ideas and information through virtual networks. This category of data is constantly evolving with the development of new social media platforms, and collection methods for the various types of social media will vary. (See Chapter 6 for more on social media collection.)

- **Structured database (on prem and/or cloud).** Typically categorized as quantitative data, structured data is highly organized data that is decipherable by proprietary software. Information for structured databases can be hosted internally on a server or remotely in the cloud. Examples include SQL databases and POS data.
- **Third-party collaboration applications (Slack, Microsoft Teams, Google Workspace).** Communication platforms and collaboration hubs that includes instant messaging, voice and video calls, and tools to help groups share information and work together.
- **Third-party messaging applications (WhatsApp, Facebook Messenger).** An application other than text messaging that allows for individuals to messages each other.

In Polly's lawsuit, we have some very clear sources of information, including email (both server based and web-based), text messages, Slack messages, maybe some social media, and potentially some data housed on Corporate Company's network servers.

III. Interviews

The purposes of conducting interviews of both the client's IT staff as well as potential custodians is to identify the potential sources of relevant data and to be able to collect this data in a defensible manner. Entering into interviews with potential custodians as well as your client's IT staff, you should have the following goals in mind:

- Identify the main sources of ESI that are most often requested in discovery;
- Understand the company's policies on BYOD, Acceptable Use, Records and Information Management, etc. (see Chapter 2 for more information on these policies);
- Learn whether individuals can store information on local hard drives;
- Identify the retention period for each system/type of ESI;
- Identify any legacy data systems that are no longer active but that house potentially responsive data;
- Identify the date range of information available in each system;
- Identify any cloud based services used and determine the process for obtaining this information;
- Identify any implicated social media and create a plan for gathering this data;

- Identify whether any information is stored with a third party or housed in an off-site storage location;
- Identify any hard copy documents the custodian may have.

This is, of course, not an exhaustive list, but it should give you the overarching and main goals to keep in mind as you enter into custodial and IT interviews.

A. Custodial Interview

A custodial interview involves asking questions to people who may have documents relevant to litigation. The questions asked focus on where to find the documents, what they might contain and what sources they may come from. (See the robust custodial interview form in the appendix.)

Note that a portion of the custodial interview focuses on the issuance of a litigation hold, asking the question of whether ESI has been appropriately preserved in the face of litigation. The next chapter will discuss the legal hold process, and the issuance of litigation holds can occur concurrently with the custodial interviews.

B. IT Interviews

An IT interview is an integral part of the discovery process, enabling you to discuss with the individual most intimately involved with your client's systems exactly how data is maintained, archived, and/or ultimately deleted.

The following is a non-exhaustive list of key terms that you should familiarize yourself with prior to conducting your IT interview. These terms, combined with the terms already defined in this book, will provide a solid basis from which you can conduct your interview to understand, at a minimum, which applications and programs are used, how and where data is stored, how long it is retained, and whether backup stores of data exist. The answers to these questions can help facilitate the collection of this data either through the client or a third-party vendor. (See Chapter 6 for more information on data collection and the use of third-party vendors.)

- **Application software programs.** These programs have specific uses, such as processing text, calculating numbers, sending e-mail, text and instant messaging, organizing large amounts of data, etc. Application software includes word processors, spreadsheets, email, text or instant messaging software, database managers, graphics, money managers, and games. These application programs generate electronic information that is then saved in proprietary computer files, which are referred to as native files.[1]

- **Archival systems.** Long-term storage systems that host data that is no longer active.
- **Backup.** A duplicate storage copy of a computer program, disk, or data. It is made for archiving purposes or for safeguarding valuable files from loss should the active copy be damaged or destroyed.
- **Computer links/local area networks (LANs).** These are the means by which computers exchange data and talk to each other. LANS allow linked computers to share data, programs, storage, and printers. A server on a local area network (LAN) is a computer (or computers) that controls access to the network and its resources (such as hard drives, e-mail, text and instant messaging, and printers). Information on servers is generally stored on hard drives or optical disks. Depending on the type of server, they are often the targets of discovery requests because of the ESI stored on them.
- **Enterprise applications.** A large software system platform designed to operate in a corporate environment.
- **Enterprise data.** Data shared by the users of an organization, generally across departments or regions.
- **IT infrastructure.** A method of organizing the computer system and network management of an organization. It will generally reflect the organization's work processes integrated with the computer network.
- **Legacy data.** Electronic information that has been used in prior software and hardware configurations.
- **PST files.** A file format used to store items like calendar events, contacts, and email messages.
- **Shared drives.** Shared spaces where teams can easily store, search, and access their files anywhere, from any device.
- **Storage media.** Used to store data from an electronic device. Many devices today have capabilities for both fixed (internal) storage/memory and the ability to store data simultaneously, to removable storage media (including online cloud internet sites).
- **System software.** Controls and coordinates the operation of the various types of equipment and operating system in a computer.

---

1. Michael Arkfeld, Arkfeld's Best Practices Guide: Information Technology Primer for Legal Professionals (2025).

The most important type of system software is a set of programs called the operating system. The operating system controls the activity of a computer whether it is a desktop, laptop, PDA, or other type of computing device.

IV. A Note on Issues of Possession, Custody, and Control

As dictated by the Federal Rules of Civil Procedure (see Chapter 1), a party is obligated to produce relevant data that is in her possession, custody, and control. Even though e-discovery attorneys and professionals have been handling ESI since the mid- to late 1990s, the question of whether specific ESI is in the possession, custody, or control of a party remains unsettled and subject to debate, especially when these questions are asked of a corporate client in relation to data its employees possess. As you conduct interviews of custodians and understand the realm of data to be collected, you must also analyze whether you are obligated to collect this data because it is in the possession, custody, or control of your corporate client or whether this information is best sought through a subpoena.

In Polly's lawsuit, this issue is seen where Darren, while in possession of a work-issued phone, also utilizes a personal cell phone not under the governance of a BYOD policy or a policy that condones the conducting of business. Additionally, the colleague Polly complained to, as well as Polly herself, has relevant text messages, but those messages are on a personal cell phone that is subject to a BYOD policy. Whether the information on Darren's, Polly's colleague's, or Polly's phone is under control of Corporate Company for purposes of discovery is an issue that hinges on the following tests, which differ according to jurisdictions.

A. Legal Tests

The analysis of whether a party has possession or custody of potentially relevant information is typically straightforward; however, whether a party has control of documents or information has proven difficult to determine. Courts have developed three basic standards to evaluate whether an individual has control over a particular data source.

- **Legal right standard.** The legal right standard is the legal right to control or obtain the documents upon demand.[2]

2. *See In re* Bankers Trust, 61 F.3d 465, 469 (6th Cir. 1995).

- **Legal right plus notification standard.** The legal right plus notification standard states that parties must not only have the legal right to obtain the information but must notify the opposing party about potentially relevant information that is held by third parties.[3]
- **Practical ability standard.** The practical ability standard requires a party to preserve, collect, search, and produce documents and ESI irrespective of that party's legal entitlement or actual physical possession of the documents if a party has the "practical ability."[4]

While offering some guidance, these differing tests have led to a lack of clarity for lawyers that must manage discovery in multiple jurisdictions.[5]

B. Policies' Influence on Possession, Custody, and Control

While courts consider applicable legal tests when determining possession, custody, and control, they also rely on other factors, such as the policies a company may have that dictate the company's control over particular sets of data. Especially with the increase of BYOD policies (see Chapter 2), courts consider these policies in determining whether a company has possession, custody, and control over an employee's phone.[6]

---

3. Lexington Ins. Co. v. Tubbs, 2009 WL 1586862, (W.D. Tenn. June 2, 2009).

4. The Sedona Conference, *Commentary on Rule 34 and Rule 45 "Possession, Custody, or Control,"* 17 Sedona Conf. J. 467, 488 (2016). *See also* Handi-Craft v. Action Trading, S.A., 2003 WL 26098543, at *6 (E.D. Mo. Nov. 25, 2003).

5. The Sedona Conference, *Commentary on Rule 34 and Rule 45 "Possession, Custody, or Control,"* 17 Sedona Conf. J. 467, 482 (2016).

6. In *In re Pork Antitrust Litig.*, No. 18-CV-1776 (JRT/HB), 2022 WL 972401 (D. Minn. Mar. 31, 2022), the Court applied both the legal rights test and the practical ability test to find the employer was not in control of its employee's text messages. The court found the company's BYOD policy did not provide the employer with rights or ownership over the messages because the company did not require an employee to use a personally-owned phone to conduct work and the company's ability to remotely wipe an employee's phone did not give the company control over the text messages since the company also did not have the ability to access, inspect, copy, or image text messages. *See also* La Belle v. Barclays Capital Inc., 340 F.R.F. 74, 2022 WL 121065 (S.D.N.Y. Jan. 13, 2022) (evaluating the issue of possession against the backdrop of the defendant's policy that prohibited employees from discussing company business on devices without company approval). Also, in *Weisman v. Barnes Jewish Hospital*, No. 4:19-CV-00075 JAR, 2022 WL 850772 (E.D. Mo. Mar. 22, 2022), plaintiffs sought the discovery of text messages from a third-party application called Telegram and because the defendants stated they did not require this application's use and had no control or possession of messages sent and received by residents and physicians through this app, the court stated the plaintiff had not

While Polly is no longer an employee of Corporate Company, her phone and its data may have been seen as under Corporate Company's control while she was an employee under the company's BYOD policy depending on what type of access such a policy granted to Corporate Company. Similarly, Polly's colleague's phone may be subject to the same scrutiny. While Darren's company-issued phone is under Corporate Company's control, Darren's personal phone may not be seen under Corporate Company's control since there was a strict policy against the use of personal phones for work-related messages and his personal phone was not subject to the BYOD policy.

C. Social Media

While social media content, be it on X, Facebook, Instagram, or TikTok, does not technically reside on individuals' phones or computers, courts are apt to deem that individuals have possession, custody, and control of the social media accounts they maintain, for which they have credentials, or to which they have membership or access.[7]

Polly and Darren would likely both be seen as maintaining control of their respective social media accounts. Corporate Company would not likely be seen as having control of Polly's account even though she may have accessed her social media accounts on a personal phone governed by a BYOD policy. Likewise, even if Darren accessed his social media accounts on his company phone, since Darren maintains the passwords and login information for these accounts, he would likely be seen as having control over the accounts. A policy prohibiting use of social media on company-issued cell phones would help make that case stronger so

---

provided enough information to lead the court to believe the defendants had not produced all relevant documents or information within its possession.

7. *See* Alex v. KHG of San Antonio, L.L.C., No. SA-13-CA-728-OLG, 2014 WL 12489735, at *5 (W.D. Tex. Aug. 6, 2014) (finding that, though defendant could obtain a plaintiff's text messages, emails, or social media posts from third parties, plaintiffs were still required to produce those text messages, emails, and social media posts). In *In re Disposable Contact Lens Antitrust*, 329 F.R.D. 336 (M.D. Fla. 2018), plaintiffs sought a motion seeking sanctions for the alleged destruction of evidence, claiming that the defendants had a duty to preserve and disclose a Facebook group that was created and administered by a third party paid consultant. Plaintiffs argued that, while the defendants did not create or administer the group, because certain employees of the defendants were members, their access established the "practical ability" to control and preserve the group's contents. The court disagreed, finding that access attributable to membership in a closed Facebook group would not suffice to confer defendants a legal entitlement to information posted by non-party members within the group.

the burden and expense of preserving and collecting the social media accounts would not be on the company's shoulders. However, if Darren accessed his social media accounts on his company-issued phone and his phone is imaged by the company during data collection, any artifacts and messages from any social media that resides on the phone itself would likely be seen in the company's possession.

Chapter 5

Preserving the Data

I. Introduction

Attorneys have an obligation to preserve data when litigation is reasonably anticipated. Preservation of data mitigates the risk that data will be erroneously destroyed, which could lead to various sanctions. (See Chapter 1 pertaining to Rule 37.) This chapter will discuss litigation holds, automatic deletion and overwrite protocols, employee departures, and other ways in which data can disappear along with how to prevent the deletion of relevant information in the face of litigation.

II. The Legal Hold

A. The Trigger

One of the principal rules of preserving data is that when an organization reasonably anticipates litigation (as either the initiator or the target of litigation), the organization has a duty to undertake reasonable actions to preserve paper documents, ESI, and tangible items that are relevant to the parties' claims and defenses and proportional to the needs of the case.[1]

The standard sounds simple enough, but the application to practice is more than ambiguous. The answer lies within the meaning of the term reasonably anticipated, and the meaning can vary from case to case. Common sense might indicate that the duty to preserve evidence is triggered when a lawsuit is filed. The fact of the matter is that the duty can arise even before a lawsuit is filed if a party is on notice that future ligation is likely.[2]

1. The Sedona Conference, *Commentary on Legal Holds, Second Edition: The Trigger & The Process*, 20 Sedona Conf. J. 341 (2019).

2. Cache La Poudre Feeds, LLC v. Land O'Lakes, Inc., 244 F.R.D. 614, 621 (D. Colo. 2007).

B. The Means

The use of a legal hold has become a common means by which organizations meet their preservation obligations. Legal holds are communications sent to individuals with potentially relevant information, placing these individuals on notice to cease any deletion or destruction of relevant material, whether automatic or manual. These communications advise of the possibility of future litigation and identify relevant documents and ESI that should be preserved. Once a notice is received, individuals should suspend standard destruction policies and implement a legal hold on all evidence that may be relevant to future litigation.

Legal holds should be issued at the first anticipation of litigation, and it is best to cast your net wide, making sure to preserve the most amount of relevant data early on, knowing that you may not collect or review all this material later on in the discovery process. But there is a delicate balance in this preservation, as unnecessarily retaining data that is not relevant or proportional to a matter can have repercussions on cost, privacy, and bandwidth. It is important to understand who the key custodians are in the matter, where data resides, and how data is managed to issue the most effective legal holds, and this understanding comes from conducting custodial and IT interviews (see Chapter 4).

In Polly's lawsuit, obvious recipients of legal holds would be Polly and Darren, but other individuals identified as key decisions makers in Polly's annual reviews and termination should also receive those holds. Additionally, the colleague that Polly texted frequently should receive notice along with colleagues that Darren texted from both of his phones to the extent those messages were relevant to the claims and issues at hand.

Sample Legal Hold Memos can be found in the appendix.

III. Best Practices for Issuing Legal Holds

While seemingly straightforward, the issuance of a legal hold does have an art to it. These are some best practices for the issuance of a legal hold:

- **Be mindful of triggering events.** Sometimes the event that triggers an organization's duty to preserve relevant ESI is obvious (e.g., a letter threatening litigation), but at other times, the event can be more subtle (e.g., employees talking to a supervisor about harassment). Be aware that the events requiring a notice are often not obvious, and it is often better to be overly proactive than to risk spoliation of relevant data.

- **Time is of the essence.** Preservation notices should be sent in a timely and expedited fashion, especially because the difference in the automated destruction of ESI versus the preservation of ESI could hinge on a few days if not a few hours.
- **Identify the recipients.** Make sure the notice is disseminated to all key players in the organization, including any assistants or personnel who may regularly handle electronic communication or filing for other individuals.
- **Identify the scope.** Be sure to be specific yet broad when defining the scope of information that could be relevant. Yes, emails are the usual target, but be sure that custodians are preserving relevant data from social media, text messages, share drives, and other messaging applications, essentially anything that is "reasonably calculated to lead to the discovery of admissible evidence."
- **Involve IT**. Identify those individuals with enterprise licenses for company systems or who maintain your client's IT infrastructure. Oftentimes, these individuals can automatically suspend auto-delete functions to prevent spoliation.
- **Put it in writing.** The legal hold notice should be sent in writing, either electronically or in paper form, so that there is a defensible audit trail documenting the hold. Verbal holds are not recommended.
- **Follow up.** Your responsibility does not end once a legal hold is issued. It is incumbent upon the attorney that she follows up with recipients to ensure continued compliance, taking time to document this check.

IV. Common Ways Data Is Deleted and How to Prevent It

A. Automatic Deletion

Due to settings a custodian may have enabled on her own device or by virtue of an employer's policy at the enterprise level, emails not otherwise saved may be automatically deleted after a specified period. Automatic deletion is often not nefarious; rather, it is a means by which a company balances the privacy protections it affords its company data with the risk that relevant data may be deleted. Additionally, automatic deletion addresses storage issues because, while storing emails is cheaper than storing physical files, storage still comes at a cost. Because these are automated procedures, it is best to disable any automatic deletion of relevant data when a legal hold is received. Disabling these automatic procedures can take a few forms and include:

- Disabling auto-delete controls set by an individual user, whether it be for email, cell phone, or other third-party applications;
- Disabling auto-delete controls set at an enterprise or company level;
- Disabling auto-deletion of relevant backups.

B. Overwrite Protocols

Overwriting protocols consist of electronic procedures whereby data is essentially destroyed when it is overwritten or copied over by other data. These procedures ensure that a company's available data space is maintained; however, in the event of a legal hold, the individual responsible for overwriting data should be notified so that relevant data is not overwritten.

C. Employee Departures

The employee offboarding process presents the risk of data destruction, as past employees' mailboxes and files may be deleted with their departures. It is imperative to have procedures and policies in place to address where data is archived and kept and for how long once an employee leaves. While companies often recycle employee devices, it is best to create a backup of devices to be kept for a specified period prior to wiping and repurposing the device. These policies and procedures are best implemented well before the thought of any litigation and should be part of a company's information governance plan (see Chapter 2 for more information).

V. Repercussions for Spoliated Data

While we discussed the repercussions for spoliated data in Chapter 1, it is worth another brief mention. If you recall, Federal Rule of Civil Procedure 37(e) dictates that sanctions be imposed for spoliated data, but the ultimate severity and imposition of these sanctions hinges on two key concepts: prejudice and intent.

If the loss of spoliated data in the normal course of business does not prejudice the requesting party, the court will likely not impose sanctions. However, if a party is prejudiced by the lack of this data, the court will take measures to cure the prejudice, whether that be via an adverse inference or something more severe. More importantly, if the court finds that the intent of the producing party was to deprive the requesting party of the data, the court could impose anything from an adverse inference, an adverse jury instruction, or even the entry of a default judgment.[3]

3. Federal Rule of Civil Procedure 37(e) states:

If electronically stored information that should have been preserved in the anticipation or conduct of litigation is lost because a party failed to take reasonable steps to preserve it, and it cannot be restored or replaced through additional discovery, the court:

(1) upon finding prejudice to another party from loss of the information, may order measures no greater than necessary to cure the prejudice; or

(2) only upon finding that the party acted with the intent to deprive another party of the information's use in the litigation may:

(A) presume that the lost information was unfavorable to the party;

(B) instruct the jury that it may or must presume the information was unfavorable to the party; or

(C) dismiss the action or enter a default judgment.

Chapter 6

Collecting the Data

Technical expertise provided by Stephen Johnson

I. Introduction

Now that data has been identified through custodial and IT interviews and been appropriately preserved, it is time to collect the data. This chapter will discuss how to collect the data and in what form the data can—and should—be collected.

It is best to envision the steps between collection and ultimate production as a funnel. That is to say, the amount of data that is ultimately identified and collected will be significantly larger than the amount that is ultimately produced.

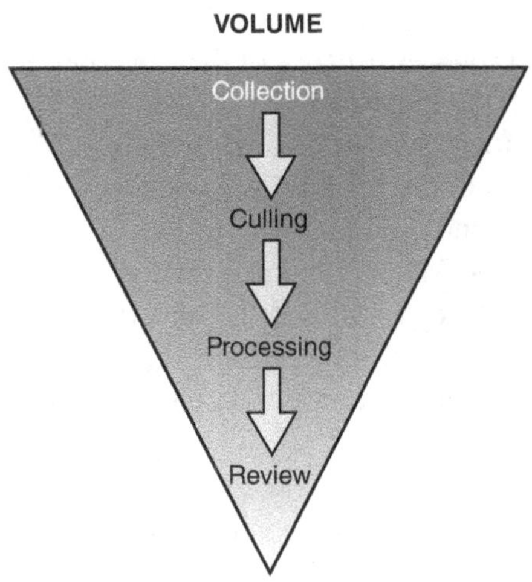

Figure 6.1. Details how broad data collections are ultimately whittled down so that only the most relevant data is produced.

II. Who Should Collect?

Data collection can be undertaken by either the client/possessor of data or a third-party vendor specializing in electronic discovery. The discussion that follows offers information about the pluses and minuses of both options.

A. Client Collection

Self-collection is a concept that often worries e-discovery professionals. Collection of ESI is generally hard because figuring out how to identify sources of information as well as how to craft search terms or other filters to pull data is challenging. There are risks associated with allowing your client to decide what ESI should be collected without the supervision or participation of counsel.[1] They include:

- **Weak or non-existent chain of custody.** IT people and other non-experienced digital evidence professionals are generally not sensitive to the chain of custody of potential evidence. This can cause inadmissibility of the evidence in court.
- **Spoliation and tampering.** Spoliation of electronic evidence will result in inadmissibility of the evidence in court. Worse than that, it can damage a corporation's reputation for not being able to conduct proper evidence preservation. (For more on spoliation and the sanctions that can occur from it, see Chapters 1 and 5).
- **Overlooked data.** Novices in data collection tend to overlook certain data sources because of their inexperience with data identification and collection.
- **Inferior tools, methods, and training**. Tools used must be tested and validated for litigation purposes. IT staff often use flawed approaches and inferior tools.
- **Inherent bias.** When a client's own staff conducts the process, there is a tendency for bias in the selection of data to be collected. Hiring an objective, uninterested third party largely eliminates the chance of inherent bias and conflict of interest.

B. Vendor Engagement

There is a myriad of e-discovery vendors that are available to assist in the collection of client data. In choosing a vendor, be sure to hire one that

---

1. Applicable case law informs that "self-collection by a layperson or information on an electronic device is highly problematic and raises a real risk that data could be destroyed or corrupted." *In re* Abilify, (Aripiprazole) Prod. Liab. Lit., 2017 WL 9249652 (N.D. Fla. 2017).

will give you the amount of support you need, the tools you require, and a price that is acceptable. As such, when hiring a vendor, take the following into consideration[2]:

- **Vendor capabilities.** Be sure that the vendor you choose is able to assist you in all areas of the EDRM that you will need help with, from collection to data processing, implementing filters, conducting of search terms, etc., through to ultimate production.
- **Vendor background.** Consider the number of years the company has been in business, their reputation with other firms or colleagues, their presence in your legal market, their reputation for security, and the responsiveness of their personnel.
- **Client capabilities.** Assess your own client's capabilities (i.e., are they technologically proficient enough to run search terms across email boxes and do they have the time to do this) to determine which vendor capabilities you may or may not need to consider.

III. How to Collect from Various Sources

Different data sources may require different collection methods. The following gives an overview of how different types of data can be collected. Note that there are often in-person as well as remote methods for these collections, and where applicable, these options are detailed below.

A. Email

Email collection can vary based on whether the account is an individual account or an enterprise/corporate account. Luckily, many email platforms have built-in capabilities to assist in data collection. Here are two common email platforms that offer built-in capabilities as well as some more information about forensic collections by a vendor.

- **Office365.** Microsoft offers e-discovery features that allow an individual or administrator to export a custodian inbox in a reviewable .PST format.
- **Gmail**. At the enterprise level, Google has a tool called Google Takeout, which can be used across Google Workplace to export data and perform basic searches.
- **Forensic collection by a vendor.** Forensic collections are typically done by a vendor and involve the extraction of email data in a forensically sound and defensible manner. The primary goal

2. *See also* The Sedona Conference, *Guidance for the Selection of Electronic Discovery Providers*, 18 SEDONA CONF. J. 55 (2017).

of this process is to maintain the integrity of the information you want to collect, including preservation of metadata. Oftentimes, email can be collected remotely by a vendor. Your client may need to provide his username and password to the vendor in order to effectuate the transfer; however, if your client is concerned about security, there are methods by which vendors can liaise with clients for their remote input of a password. Additionally, clients may need to be available to provide two-factor authentication codes, often sent to the clients' mobile devices or email addresses, to the extent this has been configured.

B. Cell Phones

Mobile devices contain a plethora of information ranging from call logs to text messages, from email to social media, so the collection of this valuable data is often critical to discovery. There are two ways that data can be collected from a cell phone:

- **Forensic collection.** This method utilizes forensic software, typically through a vendor, to recover data from a mobile device in a defensible manner. This method of collection preserves the underlying metadata; however, the client may need to surrender his phone for several hours to the forensic examiner. Sometimes, forensic cell phone collections can be accomplished by creating a backup image of the phone and transferring that image via a Secure FTP site or an encrypted drive.
- **Self-collection.** While not a defensibly sound manner of collecting data because it does not preserve the underlying metadata, self-collection of cell phone data can be accomplished through forwarding relevant information or the taking of screenshots. While these methods are not best practices, this may be used as a one-off solution for smaller cases or when collecting from a third party or a non-party.

C. Social Media

The collection of data from various social media platforms will often be dictated by the capabilities of that platform. With this caveat in mind, there are several ways that social media data can be collected:

- **Forensic collection**. As with cell phones, this method utilizes forensic software, typically through a vendor, to recover data from a particular social media platform while maintaining the defensibility and metadata of the collection. Typically, as with forensic email collection, these collections can be done remotely and often require the cooperation of the client to provide passwords and two-factor authentication where necessary.

- **Platform collection.** Some social media platforms provide downloadable versions of account activity directly from the platform. For example, Facebook and X provide the ability to download account activity under Download Your Information and Twitter Archive, respectively.
- **Screenshots.** While not a defensibly sound manner of collecting data, self-collection of social media data can be accomplished through the taking of screenshots, though the accuracy and validity of these screenshots can be called into question.

D. Slack, Teams, and Other Messaging Platforms

As with social media, for messaging platforms, the type of collection method will be tailored to the messaging platform you are collecting. Note that this area is always changing, and as applications develop, so too may the ease with which data can be collected from these applications. Some common messaging applications and their collection methods are as follows:

- **Slack.** The type of Slack plan you hold typically dictates how information can be retrieved. All workplace administrators and owners can export data from public channels; however, the same is not true for private channels and direct messages. To access records from private channels and direct messages on a free or Pro plan, you have to request this information from Slack itself. On the other hand, Business+ Workspace Owners and Enterprise Grid Org Owners can apply to access a self-serve data export.
- **Microsoft Teams.** Microsoft has made the collection of Teams messages much easier with the creation of its Core eDiscovery tool. Through this tool, admins can specify the content that they want to retrieve and export the data in various formats.
- **Signal.** The Signal support page does provide some guidance for creating backups, but these backups are able to be opened only by the application itself on either a phone or the desktop application. Although processing tools are continuously developing,

currently, there may be difficulty parsing the data meaningfully from a Signal backup because of the encryption keys Signal uses in its application.

IV. What to Collect

Best practices dictate casting a wide collection net so that data is preserved and so that you do not have to continually hound your client with new data collection requests. While the net should be cast wide, there are means by which you can cull down collection efforts from the start. During ESI protocol negotiations and the Rule 26(f) conference, parties typically decide on a list of custodians, a relevant time period, and, oftentimes, relevant search terms to be employed. Some internal email collection tools and forensic tools have capabilities to limit collections to particular custodians, timeframes, and even search term hits. As such, a more tailored data set can be culled at or near the collection stage, which ultimately saves the client money at the processing and/or review stage. If culling is not employed by these methods at the collection stage, the use of date ranges, custodians, and search terms can be later employed before data is processed and ultimately reviewed in a review platform. (See Chapters 7 and 8 on culling at the processing and review stages.)

V. How to Receive Data Securely

While it may seem easiest to merely zip up a folder of documents in a regular email for a client to send to his attorney, this method exposes data to significant risk because email is not a secure channel for sending data. Additionally, data should never be placed on an open share site. Instead, data transfers should be done through secure FTPs or encrypted hard drives, thumb drives, discs, etc.

- **Secure FTP.** SFTP or Secure File Transfer Protocol is a file transfer protocol that uses specific encryption to transfer files securely between systems. Many organizations have an SFTP already set up through which data can be shared and received. For large amounts of data, an SFTP may not be the swiftest option on a slow internet connection.
- **Encrypted hard drive or thumb/USB drive.** Drive encryption is a technology that places data on hard drives, thumb drives, or discs so that the data cannot be read by anyone who does not have access

to the appropriate key or password. When shipping an encrypted hard drive, be sure to send it via a reputable carrier and require a signature for receipt so that its delivery can be tracked.

VI. Cost Shifting for Inaccessible Data

While relevant data is commonly found with moderate effort, there is the rare occasion when data is extremely hard to retrieve. Some possible reasons why data may be hard to retrieve is that the data may be archived and stored on servers that are not readily accessible, or archival data that needs to be restored will take a significant amount of time and cost.

If you find that data is going to be hard and expensive to retrieve, the first step is to determine if there is an alternative and accessible way to retrieve the data. If there is not, the next step is to email opposing counsel and ask if they really want the data. Explain the time and cost associated with the data retrieval and ask if they are willing to pay the price to get it. If they say yes, then proceed with the data retrieval. If they say no, then you may file a motion with the court showing why the data is not proportional to the needs of the case. Additionally, you may argue that cost shifting is appropriate if the data is truly crucial to the needs of the case.

When data is requested and it is very difficult to retrieve, you may consider petitioning the court for cost shifting so that the cost associated with the retrieval of this data is placed on the requesting party. The court employs a seven-factor test to determine whether the cost of producing inaccessible data should be shifted to the party who requested it.[3] The factors the court considers are:

1. how narrowly tailored the request is to finding discoverable data,
2. the availability of the data from alternative sources,
3. the cost of producing the data compared to the amount in controversy,
4. the cost of producing the data compared to each party's resources,
5. each party's ability to control the costs of production and incentive to do so,
6. how important the issues in the litigation are, and
7. how producing the data will benefit each party.

3. Zubulake v. UBS Warburg LLC, 217 F.R.D. 309 (S.D.N.Y. 2003).

Chapter 7

Processing the Data

Technical expertise provided by Stephen Johnson

I. Introduction

Now that you have the data, how do you process it into a review platform that will help you quickly find the most relevant documents? This chapter will discuss best methods for processing data into an appropriate review space, including available platforms and the use of a universal time standard.

II. The Process of Processing

During processing into an e-discovery review platform, individual files are extracted from container files, or from loose natives in folders, and attachments and embedded objects are extracted from individual files. A container file is a single file that contains one or more other files. Examples include ZIP and PST files.[1] Each extracted item is saved as a separate file though the container file itself is not saved as a separate item.

Each extracted file is assigned a unique document identifier (document ID), often made up of numbers, letters or a combination of the two. Although attachments and embedded objects are extracted as separate files, those separate files link back to their parent files via the Group Identifier or family field.

---

1. Since most email boxes are compressed and packaged as PSTs, it is important to note that data sizes typically increase after container files are uncompressed during processing. This is important to keep in mind if you are working with an e-discovery vendor to process data, since processing is often charged on a per GB basis.

III. Culling Down the Data Set during Processing

In order to minimize the ultimate realm of documents you may be reviewing at the onset, it is appropriate to employ several measures at the processing stage to cull down your document set.

A. De-Duplication

It is common to have duplicate copies of the same document in a collected document set. Secondary copies can be removed so that only one copy remains[2] while maintaining information about which custodians had a copy of the document. This process is referred to as de-duplication. There are several types of de-duplication.

- **Global de-duplication.** This process compares an incoming document against every other document within the group of data it is part of, and all other documents in a review workspace.
- **Custodial de-duplication.** This process compares an incoming document against every other document within the custodian's group of data, and all documents already in a review platform for a given custodian. This method will leave copies in each custodian's processed mailbox but not leave multiple copies in each custodian's mailbox.

B. De-NISTing

De-NISTing is a process that removes irrelevant files from the processing set, reducing the size of any given collection. Essentially, any file type that is on the NIST list[3] will be excluded from processing. Examples of file types removed during de-NISTing are files used to execute computer programs, help files, and font files.

---

2. A computer file has a signature known as a hash value. If two files have the same hash value, they are considered to be duplicates. It is on this value that documents are de-duplicated.

3. The National Institute of Standards and Technology (NIST) maintains a list that is updated four times a year and is part of the National Software Reference Library Project. When software is used to de-NIST, the software compares all ESI in a collection against the National Software Reference Library list and removes files matching those on the list unlikely to contain relevant information. *See What Does DeNIST Mean and Why Should You Care?*, PERCIPIENT, https://percipient.co/denist-mean-care.

C. Reporting

Once data is processed, reports that show the various types of data in a review platform can be created. These reports can be used to determine which files need to be included in a review set and which can be left out. Additionally, reports can often show holes in data, identifying missing data from particular time periods or custodians. Finally, reports, specifically STRs or Search Term Reports, can show a review team which documents hit on particular search terms to help refine search terms. (See Chapter 8 for more on the development of search terms.) These reports will ultimately help a case team cull down a data set at the review stage.

D. Time Period

If a specified time period was not employed during collection, and data outside of the relevant time period was collected, a specific time period can be employed during processing to limit the amount of data that is ultimately ingested into a review platform.

IV. Time Zone Considerations

Most electronic data is stored in UTC (Coordinated Universal Time). Having time normalized in a standard time zone for all data processed is a critical aspect of data processing. Differing time zones can result in ineffective de-duplication and confusion for reviewers, especially if the time of an email is particularly important for a review. Be sure to specify in your ESI protocol the time zone in which data should be processed.

V. Processing Metadata Fields

Documents and data typically have hundreds of metadata fields associated with them. While certain metadata fields are commonly processed, it is helpful to know which metadata fields are available as some may prove useful in sorting the data for your matter. For example, the Date Created metadata field may be particularly useful if the timing of a particular contract's creation is at issue in a matter. It is also important to note that metadata information may be changed if a document is dragged, dropped, opened, or saved after its collection. That is why forensic collection along with appropriate processing of data directly into an appropriate review platform is essential to maintaining a document's metadata.

Lastly, throughout our discussion of metadata, be mindful that relevant metadata fields may be withheld or redacted according to assertions of privilege or confidentiality. We will remind you again of this topic in Chapter 9, which discusses the steps to take prior to production of data.

A. Metadata Fields Needed for Processing Data

A key list of metadata fields needed to process data into a review workspace is as follows[4]:

Processing Field Name	Field Type	Description
Container Extension	Fixed-Length Text	Document extension of the container file in which the document originated.
Container ID	Fixed-Length Text	Unique identifier of the container file in which the document originated. This is used to identify or group files that came from the same container.
Container Name	Fixed-Length Text	Name of the container file in which the document originated.
Custodian	Single Object	Custodian associated with (or assigned to) the processing set during processing.
Common Custodians	Choice	The list of all custodians who have this email.
Extracted Text	Long Text	Complete text extracted from content of electronic files or OCR data field. This field holds the hidden comments of MS Office files.
Last Published On	Date	Date on which the document was last updated via re-publish.
Level	Whole Number	Numeric value indicating how deeply nested the document is within the family. The higher the number, the deeper the document is nested.
Originating Processing Set	Single Object	The processing set in which the document was processed.
Originating Processing Data Source	Single Object	A single object field that refers to the processing data source.
Processing Duplicate Hash	Fixed-Length Text	Identifying value of an electronic record that is used for de-duplication during processing.

4. This list has been adapted from *ERDM Processing Standards Guide, Version 1*, https://edrm.net/resources/frameworks-and-standards/edrm-model/edrm-stages-standards/edrm-processing-standards-guide-version-1/.

Processing Field Name	**Field Type**	**Description**
Processing File ID	Fixed-Length Text	Unique identifier of the document in the processing engine database.
Processing Errors	Multiple Object	Any associated errors that occurred on the document during processing. This field is a link to the associated Processing Errors record.
Relativity Native Time Zone Offset	Whole Number	The hour offset based on the Time Zone ID. Numeric field that controls how header dates and times appear for email messages in the viewer or on redacted or highlighted images. This does not modify actual metadata associated with the displayed values.
Relativity Native Type	Fixed Length Text	The type of native file loaded into the system.
Supported By Viewer	Boolean	Yes/No field that indicates whether the native document is supported by the viewer.
Time Zone Field	Single Object	Indicates which time zone is used to display dates and times on a document image.
Virtual Path	Long Text	Folder structure and path to file from the original location identified during processing.

1. Why Collecting These Metadata Fields Is Necessary for a Workspace

Having these metadata fields available for processing into a review workspace is important because it ensures that documents (i.e., emails and attachments) are tied together in a unit. To be able to process data into a review platform, you must map the fields for that piece of the application prior to processing. If fields are not mapped, those fields will not get populated. Additionally, these fields help paint a picture of what type of document is being reviewed, where the documents came from (i.e., PST, MBOX, ZIP, RAR), who the document came from, what the time zone of the document was, the path where the file existed, and the text that can be searched with key terms. These fields also allow for more detailed searching and filtering.

2. What to Do If You Can't Get These Metadata Fields

If metadata fields are missing, it is best to first go back to the producing party and ask for a corrected production complete with appropriate metadata. If this request is still not successful, this is not a death knell for your review. It may just become a bit more challenging to complete advanced searching. In this instance, though inefficient with regard to time and cost, it may be worth having data reviewers code fields either prior to or during review so that data is manually entered and can then be queried.

B. Other Optional Metadata Fields

In addition to the above, other optional metadata fields are available.[5] While this list is fairly comprehensive, note that not all metadata fields are exchanged in litigation, oftentimes because a particular metadata field simply does not exist for a particular set of data. The cost associated with gathering more or less metadata fields should not vary widely, so long as the metadata is readily available and does not have to be gathered from an otherwise inaccessible source.

The particular metadata fields you are interested in will change according to the matter, and the fields that are to be exchanged are typically negotiated and set forth in an ESI protocol. Those fields that are fairly common and useful to exchange in general have been noted with an asterisk (*) below.

Processing Field Name	Field Type	Description
Attachment Document IDs	Long Text	Attachment document IDs of all child items in family group, delimited by semicolon, only present on parent items.
Attachment List	Long Text	Attachment file names of all child items in a family group, delimited by semicolon, only present on parent items.
Author*	Fixed-Length Text	Original composer of document or sender of email message.
BCC Address	Long Text	The full SMTP value for the email address entered as a recipient of the Blind Carbon Copy of an email message.
CC Address	Long Text	The full SMTP value for the email address entered as a recipient of the Carbon Copy of an email message.
Child MD5 Hash Value	Long Text	Attachment MD5 hash value of all child items in a family group, only present on parent items. Note: This value is not populated if your processing server is FIPS compliant.

5. This list has been adapted from *EDRM Processing Standards Guide, Version 1*, https://edrm.net/resources/frameworks-and-standards/edrm-model/edrm-stages-standards/edrm-processing-standards-guide-version-1/.

Processing Field Name	Field Type	Description
Child SHA1 Hash Value	Long Text	Attachment SHA1 hash value of all child items in a family group, only present on parent items.
Child SHA256 Hash Value	Long Text	Attachment SHA256 hash value of all child items in a family group, only present on parent items.
Comments	Long Text	Comments extracted from the metadata of the native file.
Company	Fixed-Length Text	The internal value entered for the company associated with a Microsoft Office document.
Contains Embedded Files	Yes/No	The yes/no indicator of whether a file such as a Microsoft Word document has additional files embedded in it.
Control Number Beg Attach	Fixed-Length Text	The identifier of the first page of the first document in a family group. This is used for page-level numbering schemes.
Control Number End	Fixed-Length Text	The unique identifier of the last page of a document. This is used for page-level numbering schemes.
Control Number End Attach	Fixed-Length Text	The identifier of the last page of the first document in a family group. This is used for page-level numbering schemes.
Conversation	Long Text	Normalized subject of email messages. This is the subject line of the email after removing the RE and FW that are added by the system when emails are replied to or forwarded.
Conversation Family	Fixed-Length Text	Relational field for conversation threads. This is a 44-character string of numbers and letters that is created in the initial email.
Conversation Index	Long Text	Email thread created by the email system. This is a 44-character string of numbers and letters that is created in the initial email and has 10 characters added for each reply or forward of an email.
Date Created*	Date	Date and time from the Date Created property extracted from the original file or email message.
Date Last Modified*	Date	Date and time from the Modified property of a document, representing the date and time that changes to the document were last saved.

Processing Field Name	Field Type	Description
Date Last Printed	Date	Date and time that the document was last printed.
Date Received*	Date	Date and time that the email message was received (according to original time zones). This applies to emails only; this field is not populated for loose files.
Date Sent*	Date	Date and time that the email message was sent (according to original time zones). This applies to emails only; this field is not populated for loose files.
Delivery Receipt	Yes/No	Indicates whether a delivery receipt was requested for an email.
Document Class	Single Choice	This field can be one of Email, Edoc, or Attach.
Document Extension*	Fixed-Length Text	Character extension of the document that represents the file type to the Windows Operating System. Examples are PDF, DOC, or DOCX.
Document Subject*	Long Text	Subject of the document extracted from the properties of the native file.
Domains (Email BCC)	Multiple Object	Domains of 'Blind Carbon Copy' recipients of the email message. See the Note below.
Domains (Email CC)	Multiple Object	Domains of 'Carbon Copy' recipients of the email message. See the Note below.
Domains (Email From)	Multiple Object	Domains of Originator of the email message. See the Note below.
Domains (Email To)	Multiple Object	Domains of 'To' recipients of the email message. See the Note below.
Email BCC*	Long Text	Recipients of 'Blind Carbon Copies' of the email message.
Email Categories	Long Text	Category/categories assigned to an email message.
Email CC*	Long Text	Recipients of 'Carbon Copies' of the email message.
Email From*	Fixed-Length Text	Originator of the email message.
Email In Reply To ID	Long Text	The internal metadata value within an email for the reply-to ID.
Email Store Name	Fixed-Length Text	The identifier of the top-level container of an email message. For example, jdoe.nsf. If a document comes from a rar/zip file attached to the email, the container is referred to in that file.

Processing Field Name	Field Type	Description
Email Subject*	Long Text	Subject of the email message.
Email To*	Long Text	List of recipients or addressees of the email message.
File Name*	Fixed-Length Text	The original name of the file.
File Size	Decimal	Generally, a decimal number indicating the size in bytes of a file.
File Type*	Fixed-Length Text	Description that represents the file type to the Windows Operating System. Examples are Adobe Portable Document Format, Microsoft Word 97 – 2003 Document, or Microsoft Office Word Open XML Format.
From Address	Long Text	The full SMTP value for the sender of an email message.
Group Identifier	Fixed-Length Text	Group the file belongs to (used to identify the group if attachment fields are not used).
Has Hidden Data	Yes/No	Indication of the existence of hidden document data such as hidden text in a Word document, hidden columns, rows, or worksheets in Excel, or slide notes in PowerPoint.
Importance	Single Choice	Notation created for email messages to note a higher level of importance than other email messages added by the email originator.
Keywords	Long Text	The internal value entered for keywords associated with a Microsoft Office document.
Last Accessed Date/Time	Date	The date and time at which the loose file was last accessed.
Last Saved By	Fixed-Length Text	The internal value indicating the last user to save a document.
Last Saved Date/Time	Date/Time	The internal value entered for the date and time at which a document was last saved.
Lotus Notes Other Folders	Long Text	A semi-colon delimited listing of all non-primary folders that a Lotus Notes message or document was included.
MD5 Hash*	Fixed-Length Text	Identifying value of an electronic record that can be used for de-duplication and authentication generated using the MD5 hash algorithm.
Meeting End Date/Time	Date/Time	The date and time at which a meeting item in Outlook or Lotus Notes ended.

Processing Field Name	**Field Type**	**Description**
Meeting Start Date/Time	Date/Time	The date and time at which a meeting item in Outlook or Lotus Notes began.
Message Header	Long Text	The full string of values contained in an email message header.
Message ID	Fixed-Length Text	The message number created by an email application and extracted from the email's metadata.
Message Type	Single Choice	Indicates the email system message type. Possible values include Appointment, Contact, Distribution List, Delivery Report, Message, or Task. The value may be appended with '(Encrypted)' or 'Digitally Signed' where appropriate.
Native File	Fixed-Length Text	The path to a copy of a file for loading into Relativity.
Number of Attachments	Whole Number	Number of files attached to a parent document.
OCR Text	Yes/No	The yes/no indicator of whether the extracted text field contains OCR text.
Office Document Manager	Fixed-Length Text	The internal value entered for the manager of a document.
Office Revision Number	Fixed-Length Text	The internal value for the revision number within a Microsoft Office document.
Other Props	Long Text	Metadata extracted during processing for additional fields beyond the list of processing fields available for mapping. This includes TrackChanges, HiddenText, HasOCR, and dates of calendar items. Field names and their corresponding values are delimited by a semicolon.
Parent Document ID	Fixed-Length Text	Document ID of the parent document. This field is only available on child items.
Password Protected	Single Choice	Indicates the documents that were password protected. It contains the value Decrypted if the password was identified, Encrypted if the password was not identified, or no value if the file was not password protected.
Primary Date	Date	Date taken from Email Sent Date, Email Received Date, or Last Modified Date in the order of precedence.
Read Receipt	Yes/No	Indicates whether a read receipt was requested for an email.

Processing Field Name	Field Type	Description
Sensitivity	Single Choice	The indicator set on an email to denote the email's level of privacy.
SHA1 Hash	Fixed-Length Text	Identifying value of an electronic record that can be used for de-duplication and authentication generated using the SHA1 hash algorithm.
SHA256 Hash	Fixed-Length Text	Identifying value of an electronic record that can be used for de-duplication and authentication generated using the SHA256 hash algorithm.
Sort Date*	Date	Date taken from the Date Sent field on email messages repeated for the parent document and all child items to allow for date sorting. For loose files (non-emails) that do not contain a specific Date Sent property, Relativity populates this field with the value that appears in that file's Modified property.
Speaker Notes	Yes/No	The yes/no indicator of whether a PowerPoint file has speaker notes associated with its slides.
To Address	Long Text	The full SMTP value for the recipient of an email message, for example, bob@example.com.
Track Changes	Yes/No	The yes/no indicator of whether tracked changes exist in the document.
Unified Title	Long Text	Subject of the document. If the document is an email, this field contains the email subject. If the document is not an email, this field contains the document's file name. This field in tandem with Group Identifier helps alleviate the problem of non-sequential control numbers within families.
Unprocessable	Yes/No	The yes/no value indicating if a file was able to be processed. If the file could not be processed, this field is set to Yes.
Unread Flag	Yes/No	Indicates whether an email was not read.

1. Why Collecting These Optional Metadata Fields Is Helpful in a Workspace

Having these optional metadata fields available in a review workspace is important because it enables a user to conduct advanced searches across fields of interest. Metadata also provides context that helps a reviewing attorney understand the relevance of a particular data set and guides them on how to use it.

For example, in Polly's case, culling emails to those from Polly Plaintiff to a particular co-worker to whom she was known to complain, or from Darren Defendant to a co-worker to whom he was known to gossip about Polly, would be particularly helpful. When metadata fields are populated, a search for emails to/from these relevant individuals is made much easier because targeted searches in the "email to" and "email from" fields can be completed. If these metadata fields are missing, that task becomes much more challenging.

2. What to Do If You Can't Get These Optional Metadata Fields

There are a variety of reasons as to why metadata may be unavailable, including that it does not exist for the document because it is a hard copy scan, a corrupt file, system file, or proprietary file type. Regardless of the reason, not having the above metadata fields will pose challenges. Documents may be searchable via OCR text-recognition; however, more nuanced searches across the metadata fields will not be feasible.

But while not having metadata fields does pose these challenges, it is not a complete impediment to your discovery process. Documents can still be searched via simple text searches when searchable text exists, either inside or outside of a workspace. While this may not be the most efficient way to review and cull a document set, you can at least quickly apply key terms to identify a document's usefulness.

VI. Problems with Processing

When processing files, there are a variety of hiccups that can occur along the way. Here are just a few to remember before your next processing job:

- **Password-protected or encrypted files.** Sometimes items can be password protected. While it is ideal to have documents received in an unlocked state, there are many types of software that can crack passwords. Also, many processing tools allow you to input passwords so documents can be unlocked during processing.
- **Corrupt files.** These are files that have structural problems that prevent them from being opened or manipulated. It is often easiest to go to the source of the document to see if an uncorrupted version of the document exists. If such a copy does not exist, steps can be taken to either repair the corrupt file or to exclude

it from production. If the document is excluded, best practices dictate that this action be documented.

- **Unprocessable files.** These are files that do not support the common e-discovery actions. For example, .db or database files are created when data is exported from a database. While these documents are necessary in the functioning of data in a database, they have no real function or processable document equivalent in a review workspace. As such, these files will likely not make their way into a review workspace but their absence should not pose an impediment to document review.

Regardless of glitches that may occur in your process, it is important that all exceptions be logged and documented.

VII. Ingesting Data into a Review Workspace

Data ingestion is a process by which data is received and processed into a review workspace so that it can be reviewed. While one might imagine that data is simply dumped into a review workspace and then ready for review with a few clicks of a button, technologists work hard on the other end of the ingestion process to make sure it is brought into a review workspace in an appropriate format for review and to identify any problems with the data. Ample time, typically 24 hours, needs to be allotted so that your hired vendor can complete this process.

VIII. Available Review Platforms

The number of review platforms (workspaces) and companies that offer review software solutions is growing each year. There are a few well-known platforms to consider if your firm does not have its own review platform but note that this list is not exhaustive and the technology is always changing. It is best to check in with each particular platform's website for its latest capabilities and to explore demos of available products to learn more about their functionality.

The Sedona Conference has offered tremendous guidance on the selection of an electronic discovery provider.[6] In particular, it suggests

6. The Sedona Conference, *The Sedona Conference Guidance for the Selection of Electronic Discovery Providers*, 18 SEDONA CONF. J. 56–140 (2017).

having a firm grasp on the type of matter, the types and sources of ESI, the proportionality needs of the case, the cross-border nature of the data, and the time constraints posed by discovery when choosing a vendor. It also suggests defining the need for an ESI vendor, preparing market research related to vendor service options, developing a short list of main contenders, and appropriately vetting these options before proceeding. To help with this process, here are a few review platforms available for your next case:

- Relativity
- Everlaw
- Logikcull
- DISCO
- Reveal

IX. Using an Early Case Assessment (ECA) Workspace

When data is ingested into a review platform, most review platforms offer an Early Case Assessment capability to initially assess data prior to promotion to responsive review. An ECA workflow simplifies and streamlines the process of early case assessment by removing unneeded content, allowing individuals to host data at a cheaper rate while search terms are run, Search Term Reports are generated, and the ultimate composition of the data is assessed. Ultimately, the most responsive documents are promoted to responsive review, and because only a portion of data is promoted and hosted, one only pays the workspace storage fees and the promotion data charges for the smaller subset of data. It is often within the ECA that the methods for culling data down into a manageable review set detailed in the next chapter are employed.

Chapter 8

Reviewing and Analyzing the Data

Technical expertise provided by Stephen Johnson

I. Introduction

This chapter will discuss reviewing and analyzing the data, both for production and to identify key documents to use in your case, including the use of search terms, analytics (including predictive AI), and issue and confidentiality tagging.

While the receipt of Requests for Production from opposing counsel may spur your review of documents to determine what is and is not responsive to a request, you may start reviewing documents well before requests are served to know what information you have to support your claims and defenses. As such, once documents are received, and especially if the document set is large, you will likely begin to make strategic decisions as to how to cull down a data set so that you can find responsive and/or relevant documents quickly.

II. Methods for Culling Review Sets and Finding Relevant Documents

In the era of electronic discovery, review teams rarely, if ever, set eyes on every document to review (also known as a linear review). Technology is now utilized to cull document sets down to manageable chunks for review and to review inbound documents for relevant data in an efficient manner. While many of the below methods can be utilized on inbound productions from opposing counsel, they are most often employed to review documents for production. In this case, discussions around the applications of search terms and the use of technology-assisted review often take place at the Rule 26(f) conference and continue throughout discovery as both parties determine the best methods for efficiently and effectively reviewing and producing documents.

A. Search Terms

In the early stages of discovery, search terms are applied to a data set to either cull the documents down to likely relevant data or to find relevant data quickly. Terms are often drafted by the e-discovery or case team attorney and are gleaned from the conversations with the custodians, RFPs that have been exchanged, and general terms from the issues and claims in the litigation.

Note that search terms are crafted through an iterative process. Once a set of terms is crafted, a typical workflow has these keywords run through a workspace to return Search Term Reports (STRs), which quickly indicate which terms are returning the most hits, which terms are returning unique-to-that-term hits, and whether the number of hits for a particular term seems inordinate. In a situation where key terms come back with a significant amount of hits, the priority should be to address and revise those terms with a significant amount of unique hits, as this is an indication of an overlay broad term. In many cases, an inordinate number of hits may indicate that the term needs to be further refined because it is picking up the term in an area of the document that is not relevant for your purposes. These hits are often referred to as false positives. For example, looking for the term "road" may return documents that hit on "road" in an individual's email address signature but that have nothing to do with the matter at hand. In this case, further refining of the term (perhaps with Boolean connectors—see below) is warranted.

1. Keywords

A keyword search is the most obvious type of searching you can do. In fact, you likely use keywords every time you do a web-based search, and like web-based searches, search terms are input into a search function and a list of documents containing the search term is returned.

In Polly's case, keywords may have developed after Polly's custodial interview. Perhaps she mentioned that Darren often called her old or that he once asked her about early retirement, and that she complained about both comments in a text message to her colleague. "Old" and "early retirement" may be two important keywords to use while searching Polly's text messages. Note that "old" may return many false positives, as indicated above, and thus a Boolean connector (see next section) may be needed to further hone in on the relevant data.

During Darren's custodial interview, he mentioned he has emails showing that Polly was resistant to a very integral marketing campaign called Project Bulldog that was to be social media driven. Perhaps the name of the project is a keyword that should be used to search both Polly's and Darren's emails.

2. Boolean

Boolean searches are an advanced method of keyword searching and permit word and phrase combinations using operators such as AND, OR, and NOT to limit or broaden searches. These are the same searches often used with Westlaw or LexisNexis. Combinations of the below options can be strung together in a single search to formulate complex searches.

Some useful Boolean operators are:

- **AND.** Provides results that contain both or all keywords. By searching project AND bulldog, we will find all documents that contain both words regardless of their placement within the document.
- **OR.** Provides results that contain either keyword. By searching project OR bulldog, we will find all documents that contain either of those words, even if both don't appear in the same document.
- **NOT or AND NOT.** Provides results that contain the first keyword but not the second. By searching project AND NOT bulldog, we will find all documents that contain the word project but that do not contain the word bulldog. This search can be useful in weeding out documents. If, for example, Project Poodle was active at the same time as Project Bulldog, searching for project AND NOT poodle will return documents containing the word project while weeding out the documents containing the word poodle.
- **Quotation marks.** Provides results that contain the exact phrase within the quotation marks. By searching "Project Bulldog," we will find all documents that contain the exact phrase Project Bulldog, while weeding out those that only contain either word separately (e.g., someone messaging about their bulldog).
- **Parentheses.** Allows you to group keywords and control the order in which the terms are searched. By searching (project OR bulldog) AND Polly, we will find all documents that contain the word project and the word Polly, as well as all documents that contain the word bulldog and the word Polly.
- **Asterisk/wildcard characters.** Provides results that contain a variation of the keyword. By searching for terminat*, we will

find all documents that contain that root word, e.g., the words terminate, termination, and terminating. Note that some review platforms utilize different characters for this wildcard function. Consult with your vendor to determine which character to use.

- **W/number value**. Provides results where words or phrases are separated by a set number of characters either before or after the first word. For example, bull w/10 dog would provide results where the word bull is within 10 words of the word dog.

3. Fuzzy and Phonic

A fuzzy search is a search function available in many review platforms that finds words based on spelling similarities. For example, in using a fuzzy search for bulldog, you will find documents with, e.g., bulldog, bull dog, or bulldogg.

Similarly, a phonic search provides results that sound alike. A search for John will also return documents containing Jon.

4. Stemming

A stemming search returns all variations of a root word. In searching terminate with the stemming function, you will find documents containing terminating, termination, terminate, terminates, and terminated.

5. Synonym and Concept

A synonym search uses a thesaurus and returns documents containing either the search term or a synonym. These synonyms are inherent in the review platform and do not need to be provided by the attorney. Again, be aware of false positives, especially if the synonyms checked are expansive. For example, a search for terminate may also bring back documents that contain the words end, stop, or expire.

A concept search expands the search beyond the keywords chosen and returns documents relevant to the concept underlying the search terms. For example, a search for performance may also find documents that contain the words goal, evaluation, or skill.

B. Technology-Assisted Review (TAR)

Technology-assisted review (TAR) is the process of having computer software electronically classify documents based on input from reviewers. Reviewers may code documents for responsiveness, privilege, or specific issues depending on the needs of the case team. The steps of a typical TAR workflow[1] is as follows:

- **Set goals.** The case team determines the technology-assisted review process for a specific case by identifying the goals of the TAR process. Some of the goals a case team may wish to achieve are:
  a. reduction and culling of irrelevant documents;
  b. prioritization of the most substantive documents; and/or
  c. quality control of the human reviewers.
- **Set protocol and educate reviewers.** A document review protocol is given to the human reviewers (see below for more on the creation of review protocols). Aside from clarifications of responsiveness, privilege, etc., this protocol specifically addresses more nuanced points of a review, such as whether to code a family of documents consistently.
- **Code documents.** Human reviewers begin to code documents to adequately train the TAR system to understand the boundaries of a category, such as responsiveness.
- **Predict results.** The TAR system applies the information learned from the human reviewers and classifies a selected set of documents with predetermined labels.
- **Test results.** Human reviewers review a statistical sample of the TAR performance to determine the validity of its performance. Depending on the results, the reviewers may need to repeat the steps of coding documents, predicting results, and testing results until a desired threshold of performance is met.
- **Evaluate results.** Once TAR has achieved the desired threshold of performance, the case team will look at the results to determine if the TAR system has achieved the goals anticipated.

1. Continuous Active Learning

Continuous active learning (CAL) is a form of TAR that allows review to begin immediately without waiting for randomly selected sample training sets to be reviewed and tested against the total population of documents. CAL works by building a dynamic TAR model that takes into account the decisions the review team made on a seed set of documents, whether those decisions involve responsiveness, privilege, or specific issue coding.

---

1. EDRM, *Technology Assisted Review*, https://edrm.net/resources/frameworks-and-standards/technology-assisted-review.

Feedback from ongoing document review is continuously incorporated into the CAL model. When considering CAL, there are typically one of two workflows implemented: prioritized review or coverage review.

- **Prioritized review.** For a prioritized review, after the seed set is run through the workspace, the active learning tool queues up the most relevant documents to the reviewers. As the reviewers continue to code these relevant documents, more documents are then queued for review. This process continues until reviewers come to a point where only non-relevant documents are being queued up for review. At this point, the review can stop. This workflow can save time from a linear review, and it ensures that all relevant documents are brought to the forefront of the review within an acceptable margin of error.
- **Coverage review.** Coverage review queues relevant and non-relevant documents to the reviewers after a seed set is run through the workspace. As the reviewers review and tag documents as relevant or not relevant, the machine continuously learns which documents are which and identifies documents as either responsive or nonresponsive. Coverage review begins by presenting the documents the model is most unsure about (rated by a percentage) and continues until a certain percentage of confidence in the document coding is achieved. This method is often employed so that productions can be made as quickly as possible.

C. Clustering

Clustering is designed to help organize data by grouping conceptually related documents by looking at ideas and similar text patterns. When particularly hot documents are already identified, clustering can help a reviewer find other similar documents quickly and efficiently. It is especially beneficial in the early stages of a review when the team is unfamiliar with the data. By applying clustering, relevant documents can often be quickly identified so that the set requiring human review is minimized.

D. Categorization

Categorization is a process where the reviewer creates a set of example documents that analytics uses as the basis for identifying and grouping other conceptually similar documents. This is useful early in a case where understanding of certain key concepts is used to identify other documents in a universe of data that are also representative of those concepts. During review, documents could be added to various categories as examples, which can then be used to apply those categories to the larger universe of data. Whereas clustering can only place documents into one category, categorization can place a single document into numerous categories since most documents, on average, can be applied to more than one category. This is most helpful when there is one or more large volumes of discovery that you wish to categorize quickly without any user information or coding, and you have example documents for specific categories.

E. Email Threading

Email threading identifies and groups all the emails (replies, replies to all, and forwards) from a single conversation. Threading allows reviewers to see a complete email conversation as they are coding documents and obviates the need to review duplicative parts of an email chain. Additionally, since the same reviewer is coding the entire thread, it allows for consistent coding. When used in document review, the single most inclusive thread is reviewed only once, reducing the number of documents for review. For example, if Peter emails Paul, and Paul replies to that email, and then Peter responds to that reply, only the last message (Peter's response to Paul's reply) is queued for review since Peter's initial email and Paul's reply will appear underneath Peter's response. However, if Peter then forwards his response to Mary, this thread will not drop out of the review because it is unique and contains data (i.e., the forward from Peter to Mary) that the previous responses and replies do not contain. Email threading should be utilized at the earliest possible point of review to whittle down a large data set and to give the reviewer the full picture of an email exchange.

F. Near Dupes

Near dupe analytics looks at the actual text of the documents. The largest document is seen as the principal document, and a decision is made as to how similar the near dupes must be to qualify as a dupe. By highlighting the differences between documents, a reviewer does not need to reread the same content more than once; rather, the near dupes can be coded the same and only one of the dupes needs to be read. This tool is especially helpful when reviewing drafts and contracts and for performing relevancy and privilege quality control.

G. A Word about Generative Artificial Intelligence

The advent of generative artificial intelligence (GenAI) tools that are baked into many review platforms continuously changes by the day. These tools are being developed to streamline review, readily identify privileged materials, transcribe audio and visual files, automate redactions, and easily find data through queries. GenAI tools are as unique as the platforms on which they reside. It is best to check with your vendor so that you can understand these tools and, more importantly, understand how to properly use them.[2]

III. Preparing for Review

A. Review RFPs, Answers and Objections, and Other Relevant Pleadings

One of the first steps in preparing to review documents is to become familiar with the matter so that you can better understand the issues, claims, and defenses and also know how particular documents may be used to bolster these claims and/or defenses. Review of the relevant pleadings will help give appropriate background.

Additionally, it is important to review the Requests for Production served by opposing counsel and to understand how any answers or objections may impact what you will produce. In many cases, while documents may seem relevant to the underlying matter, they may be withheld if they were not requested by opposing counsel or if they fall into a category of documents to which you are objecting to producing.

One last note before we explore the practical application of the above: if you are going to use a document in your case, you must produce it. Leaving aside the fact that discovery requires that you produce relevant documents within your possession, custody, and control, if you show up at trial with an un-Bates stamped, not produced document, you will likely not be able to use it as evidence and the judge will be more than annoyed.

Consider our hypothetical case where Polly Plaintiff serves Requests for Production on Darren Defendant, asking for the following: (1) all evaluations, communications, and documents reflecting Polly's performance during her employment at Corporate Company; and (2) the complete personnel file for Polly Plaintiff. After running agreed-upon search terms, you realize that there are 500,000 documents to review that hit on the terms because, after all, Polly was employed for 10 years. Given the volume of documents

2. Lawyers' ethical duties require an understanding of AI, its use, and the implications of its use. For example, Rule 1.1 of the ABA Model Rules of Professional Conduct states "a lawyer shall provide competent representation to a client" and that this duty "requires the legal knowledge, skill, thoroughness and preparation reasonably necessary for the representation." Comment 8 to Rule 1.1 reaffirms this sentiment, stating "to maintain the requisite knowledge and skill, a lawyer should keep abreast of changes in the law and its practice, including the benefits and risks associated with relevant technology."

and the extensive period, Darren Defendant and Corporate Company may choose to object to producing all evaluations and documents reflecting her performance during her employment as unduly burdensome. They have a few alternative options. They may object and agree to produce only the documents from the year before Darren supervised Polly and the year during which he supervised her. This means that, during the review process, either through date restriction (which would be recommended) or linear review, documents that reflect Polly's performance from three years ago, while arguably relevant, would not be produced given Darren's and the Company's objection and two-year restriction. If those documents from three years ago are extremely helpful to Darren's case (i.e., they show Polly's poor performance), they may (1) choose not to object and will review and produce everything relevant from the past 10 years, or (2) choose to object to the burdensome request and produce documents from only the past three years.

B. Gather a Review Team If Necessary

While a solo attorney may choose to undertake review of documents on her own, it is common for attorneys to either gather younger associates for a large-scale document review or to hire contract attorneys from a vendor. Regardless of which review team you choose to construct, the chance of successful coding relies on a detailed review protocol as well as successful communication between the review team members.

C. Craft a Review Protocol

A review is only as good as its review protocol, but what exactly is a review protocol? A review protocol is a detailed explanation of the case's background, the relevant claims and defenses, and, most importantly, the coding fields each reviewer will be coding for. In addition, a detailed description should be included as to when particular tagging for each field should be employed. Coding fields are discussed in more detail in the next section but note that these are not hard and fast designations. Coding fields and choices can be customized to meet your particular needs for a case. See the appendix for a sample review protocol.

1. Review Coding; Responsiveness

The responsiveness field focuses on whether a document is responsive to a request for production (i.e., whether that document will ultimately be produced). There are several responsiveness designations review teams use to separate documents into those that are to be produced, those that are not to be produced, those that need to be privilege logged, or those that need a further look.

- **Responsive documents.** Documents that fall within one of the categories of responsive documents as considered by the RFPs and any objections thereto.
- **Nonresponsive documents.** Documents that do not fall within one of the below categories.
- **Withhold privilege.** Documents that fall within the privilege designation detailed below. Note that the choice to withhold a document based on privilege may be set out in a different field other than the responsiveness field. Remember that a document may be responsive, but it can still be withheld for privilege purposes.
- **Needs further review.** Documents you may want to have reviewed by another member of the case team or the lead attorney because responsiveness is not clear.
- **Technical issue.** Documents with a technical issue.

2. Confidentiality

The confidentiality field in a review layout contemplates any confidentiality orders that have been entered into. (See Chapter 3 for more on confidentiality orders.) Note that attorneys tend to overuse confidentiality, marking everything confidential when there is no particular order enforcing these designations. Be sure that your tagging comports with agreed upon confidentiality and/or protective orders. Some common confidentiality tags include:

- Confidential
- Highly confidential
- Attorneys' eyes only
- Subject to HIPAA Protective Order

3. Privilege

A more thorough discussion of privilege and when to apply particular privileges is detailed below. The most common types of privilege categories included for a document review are:

- Attorney-client communication
- Attorney work product

4. Issue Tags

Issue tags are as unique as the matter itself. These are tags that are developed by the case team so that documents, as they are reviewed, can be siloed into different categories, as either being relevant to a particular claim or defense at hand, or being supportive or non-supportive of particular claims and defenses.

If Polly Plaintiff's review team is looking at inbound documents from Darren Defendant, they may wish to silo documents into categories using the following issue tags to determine which documents show Polly's great job performance, her poor job performance, Darren's poor supervision of Polly, or his exemplary supervision of Polly:

Polly's performance – positive

Polly's performance – negative

Darren supervision – positive

Darren supervision – negative

5. Attorney Comments

The attorney comments field in a review platform is always helpful in allowing attorneys to make notes about why they feel a particular document is important, to designate certain documents for use at particular depositions, or to use particular documents in the development of a case timeline. Issue tags pertinent to individual depositions and timeline development can also be customized and created by your vendor, but the attorney review comments field is an easy way to capture relevant information fast, especially in the beginning of a review.

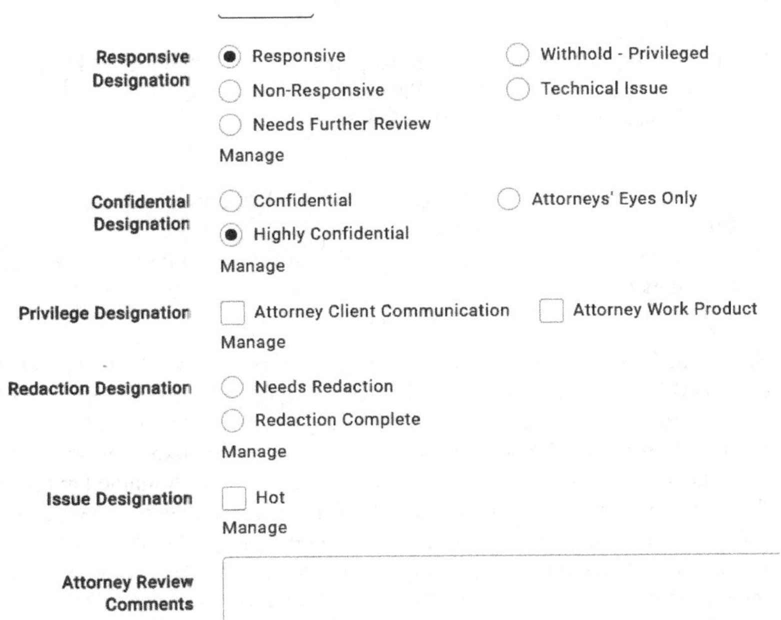

Figure 8.1. Example of a coding layout in a review platform where fields can be populated for responsiveness, confidentiality, privilege, redaction, issues, and more. Source: Relativity.

D. Review Team Communication

It is important that communication is shared amongst all review team members so that everyone is on the same page in terms of review. Creating a group email distribution list for the review is helpful, and as questions arise, circulating both the questions and answers, along with document examples, will ensure that coding is done as uniformly as possible. Keeping a log of these questions and answers will also ensure that any new review team members that are added later can easily be caught up to speed.

E. A Note on Hiring Contract Attorneys

There is a myriad of vendors who offer contract attorneys for a price per hour that is below the rate of a standard track attorney. To set yourself up for success, establish a rapport with one or two local vendors and become familiar with contract attorneys, keeping note of those who are responsive and efficient. The more you work with the same attorneys, the more they are going to understand and anticipate your needs and style for a given case. Also, in the beginning of a review, it is incumbent upon you to perform a diligent check of the attorneys' work, ensuring they are coding according to your expectations, and course correcting early on to avoid pitfalls late into the review.[3] More on quality control review follows.

---

3. Lawyers in a supervisory role are responsible for the conduct of lawyers they are supervising. *See* MODEL RULE OF PROFESSIONAL CONDUCT 5.1. Responsibilities of Partners, Managers, and Supervisory Lawyers:

* * *

> "(c) A lawyer shall be responsible for another lawyer's violation of the Rules of Professional Conduct if:
>
> the lawyer orders or, with knowledge of the specific conduct, ratifies the conduct involved"

* * *

This is true in the context of a lawyer's duty to oversee the work of contract attorneys. *See* J-M Manufacturing Co. v. McDermott Will & Emery, Superior Court of the State of California, June 02, 2011. In *J-M Manufacturing*, McDermott represented JM regarding subpoenas. They identified 160 custodians who likely had relevant ESI and ultimately produced documents to opposing counsel that contained many privileged documents. Opposing counsel asked JM to do a privileged review, followed by a subsequent document production. McDermott employed contract attorneys to conduct the review to remove all privileged documents. After the review, McDermott conducted a limited "spot-check" of the contracting attorneys' work. JM eventually retained new counsel to replace McDermott, and opposing counsel subsequently notified JM that McDermott produced 3,900 privileged documents in the latter document production. JM then filed suit against McDermott for malpractice.

IV. Quality Control (QC) Review

Even if you have a detailed review protocol, it is likely that two individuals will see a document differently. It is important to course correct early on in a review if document reviewers are coding documents differently. The best method to QC your reviewers' work is to pull a random sample (this can be anywhere from 10–15%) of reviewed documents across all reviewers or to review the entire first batch of each reviewer so that specific feedback can be provided.

If you are using a review platform, it is best to create a QC layout as you review the coded documents where any changes you make to either responsiveness, confidentiality, privilege, or even issue tags are tracked. Additionally, as you come across any coding you change, it is important to communicate not only the changes you made to the documents but also why you made those changes. This will help reviewers understand your reasoning so they can make more consistent coding decisions moving forward.

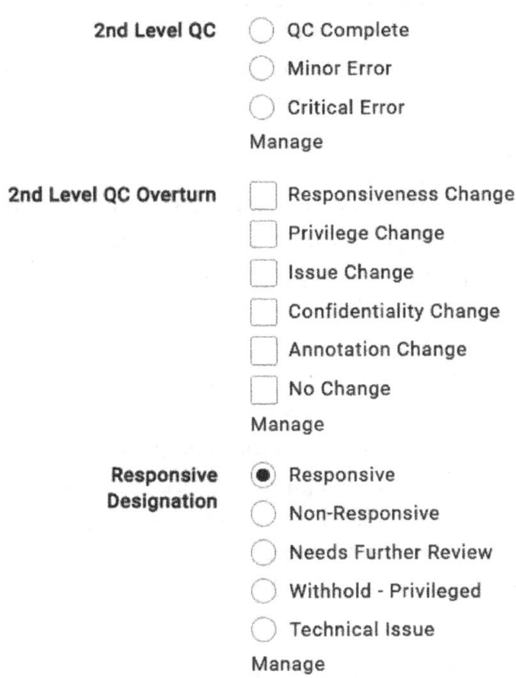

Figure 8.2. Example of a QC coding layout in a review platform where a supervisory attorney can track what was changed in a document and subsequently make any changes directly in the layout. Source: Relativity.

V. Privilege Review

Privileged documents will either need to be withheld from production to opposing counsel or redacted so that privileged information is not revealed to opposing counsel. Thus, in understanding a privilege review, it is important to know the types of privilege available to claim.

A. Types of Privilege

The two most common privileges that will necessitate either the withholding or redacting of a document are the attorney-client communication privilege and the attorney work product privilege. You should have an understanding as to when these privileges apply before applying them.

1. Attorney-Client Privilege

Under federal common law, the attorney-client privilege protects from disclosure any communications that involve only clients, their counsel, and/or certain third parties, such as client-agents and attorney-agents who may be involved without rendering the communication non-confidential. The communications must be confidential when they occur and intended to be kept confidential, and they must be made for the purpose of obtaining or rendering legal advice. This protection can be waived.

2. Work Product Doctrine

The work product privilege protects from disclosure to third parties documents and tangible things that are prepared in anticipation of litigation by (or for) another party or its representative. This privilege may be overcome in certain instances where the party seeking discovery shows that it has a substantial need for the materials to prepare its case and cannot, without undue hardship, obtain their substantial equivalent by other means. However, even if the work product protection is overcome, courts must still protect from disclosure the mental impressions, conclusions, opinions, or legal theories of a party's attorney or other representative concerning the litigation. Like the attorney-client privilege, the work product doctrine's protections may also be waived.

There are two essential types of work product that are protected from disclosure:

- **Fact work product.** Protects from disclosure documents and tangible things that are prepared both in anticipation of litigation, and by or for a party, a party's representative (such as counsel, agent, consultant, retained expert, or employer), or counsel's representative (such as an agent, consultant, or retained expert).

An opposing party may obtain fact work product if the requesting party demonstrates that it has a substantial need for the document or thing to prepare its case and cannot, without undue hardship, obtain the substantial equivalent of the document or material by other means.[4]

- **Opinion work product.** Protects from disclosure documents and tangible things that both are prepared in anticipation of litigation and by a party's counsel or other representative. This work product includes or reflects the creator's mental impressions, conclusions, opinions, and legal theories. Opinion work product may be obtained in only very limited circumstances.[5]

B. Steps for Privilege Review and Redactions

First, when utilizing e-discovery software to generate a privilege screen or log, consider three categories of privilege searches to run, and review the resultant hits:

- Generate privilege search term reports that identify all documents containing an attorney's name and quarantine those for a separate review. These lists are often gathered after speaking with a client and understanding the attorneys they may have used in the past.
- Identify all documents with law firm names or domains and quarantine those for a separate review.
- Identify all documents that contain general privilege terms such as attorney-client, legal, or attorney work product, and quarantine those for a separate review. Note that individuals often label material as privileged even when it is not, and many individuals have verbiage in their email signature about the confidentiality and privilege of the information contained therein. You may get false positives if you use the term "privilege" in your search terms, so try utilizing Boolean connectors and qualifying terms to obtain more accurate results. (See earlier for more on Boolean terms.)

Second, review the documents identified above to determine if the document is, in fact, privileged. In determining privilege, consider whether the advice given is legal advice or business advice. This

---

4. Federal Rule of Civil Procedure 26(b)(3)(A)(ii).

5. *See* United States v. Adlman, 134 F.3d 1194, 1204 (2d. Cir. 1998) (noting that a "highly persuasive showing" of need can overcome opinion work product); *but see* F.T.C. v. Boehringer Ingelheim Pharm., Inc., 180 F. Supp. 3d 1, 18 (D.D.C. 2016) (noting that opinion work product is "virtually undiscoverable").

distinction is particularly tricky when individuals in a company who are attorneys act in non-attorney roles.

Third, conduct a privilege QC by reviewing all documents that have been coded as privileged by your review team and make sure that similar or related documents are coded the same.[6] Similar documents can be found by leveraging some of the search terms and analytics tools discussed previously.

To the extent that redactions are made on partially privileged documents, be sure that those redactions comport with any agreed-upon formatting from your ESI protocol and determine whether these documents ultimately need to be included on a privilege log. So long as the reason for the redaction is apparent on its face (i.e., the redaction says either "attorney client communication" or "attorney work product") and the relevant metadata is viewable, it is most efficient to not include these on a privilege log. To the extent redactions have been made on documents reviewed in PDF format, be sure that those redactions are appropriately burned onto the PDF image and cannot be easily removed by opposing counsel.[7] Also, when redacted documents are produced, be sure that any metadata corresponding to the redacted material is redacted. (See Chapter 9 on things to consider before production.)

Finally, be sure that the appropriate information (including metadata and any manually created descriptions) that is to be included in your agreed-upon privilege log exists. Often the type of log that you agreed to in your ESI protocol will dictate which metadata fields you need to have populated.[8]

C. Privilege Logging the Data

A mere objection that a document is protected by the attorney-client privilege or work product doctrine is not sufficient to withhold a document. The objecting party must: (1) expressly claim the privilege or protection, (2) describe the nature of the withheld documents and other information in a manner that does not reveal privileged or protected information, and

6. A careless privilege review may lead to waiver of attorney-client privilege under Federal Rule of Evidence 502(b), so be sure to appropriately QC and monitor any younger attorneys or contract attorneys who may be doing the review.

7. If you happen to receive documents that are not appropriately redacted, you have an ethical duty to alert opposing counsel of the mistake. Model Rule of Professional Conduct 4.4(b).

8. Note that you can agree in your ESI protocol to not have to manually populate metadata fields. So, to the extent that metadata does not exist because of some error in processing or to the extent this information simply does not exist, the metadata does not need to be manually entered on the exported privilege log.

(3) enable other parties to assess or contest the privilege or protection claim. There are different types of privilege logs that satisfy these elements, giving opposing counsel enough information to understand the basis of why a document was withheld.

As mentioned in Chapters 1 and 3, the details of a privilege log (such as which type) are set as part of the discovery plan at your initial meet and confer or Rule 26(f) Conference. The parties should have discussed the scope of the privilege review as well as the relevant details of the log, and this should be reflected and memorialized in the ESI protocol.

1. Traditional Privilege Log

A traditional privilege log is the log most attorneys are familiar with, and it includes a detailed description of the privilege being claimed for every withheld document receiving an entry. Information that is typically included in a traditional privilege log includes:

- Bates range of each document withheld or redacted
- filename of the document
- type of document (letter, memo, report, handwritten note)
- date of document
- subject of the document
- author
- from/to/cc/bcc/recipients
- custodian
- withheld or redacted
- privilege type (e.g., attorney-client or work product)
- privilege description

When drafting privilege descriptions, it is best to describe the nature of the documents, communications, or tangible things not produced or disclosed in a manner that does not reveal information that is itself privileged or protected and that enables other parties to assess the claim. A typical description includes:

- something describing the type of document (e.g., spreadsheet, email, etc.);
- a description of the legal action (reflecting counsel's legal advice); and
- the subject matter of the document (standard operating procedures or government investigation).

The description can be typed out by a reviewer in an Excel spreadsheet or Word document, or created using fields that have been prepopulated with choices in a review platform.

Plaintiffs vs. Defendants et al.
Case 00-000-0000
Defendants' Privilege Log

Unique ID	Date	Email To	Email From	Email CC	Email Subject	File Name	Author	Privilege Type	Privilege Description
PRIV_DEF0001	11/6/2025	Larry Lawyer (llawyer@firm.com)	Debbie Defendant (ddefendant@company.com); Darren Defendant (ddef@company.com)	Amy Assistant (aassistant@company.com)	RE: Employee Evaluation for Plaintiff			Attorney Client	Email chain from Defendants to Counsel providing information so that legal advice can be rendered regarding Employee Termination
PRIV_DEF0002	11/6/2025					Employee Evaluation for Plaintiff	Debbie Defendant	Attorney Client	Attachment to email chain from Defendants to Counsel providing information so that legal advice can be rendered regarding Employee Termination
PRIV_DEF0003	11/6/2025	Debbie Defendant (ddefendant@company.com); Darren Defendant (ddef@company.com)	Larry Lawyer (llawyer@firm.com)		RE: Employee Evaluation for Plaintiff			Attorney Client/Attorney Work Product	Email chain from Defendant Counsel to Defendants providing legal advice regarding Employee Termination
PRIV_DEF0004	7/27/2025	Debbie Defendant (ddefendant@company.com); Darren Defendant (ddef@company.com)	Larry Lawyer (llawyer@firm.com)	Amy Assistant (aassistant@company.com)	RE: Employee Evaluation for Plaintiff			Attorney Client/Attorney Work Product	Email chain from Defendant Counsel to Defendants providing legal advice regarding Employee Termination
PRIV_DEF0005	7/27/2025	Larry Lawyer (llawyer@firm.com)	Debbie Defendant (ddefendant@company.com); Darren Defendant (ddef@company.com)		RE: Next Steps for Litigation			Attorney Client	Email chain from Defendants to Counsel providing information so that legal advice can be rendered regarding Employee Termination
PRIV_DEF0006	7/27/2025					Employee Previous Evaluations	Darren Defendant	Attorney Client	Attatchment to email chain from Defendants to Counsel providing information so that legal advice can be rendered regarding Employee Termination
PRIV_DEF0007	7/27/2025					Internal Email Regarding Plaintiff	Darren Defendant	Attorney Client	Attachment to email chain from Defendants to Counsel providing information so that legal advice can be rendered regarding Employee Termination

Figure 8.3. Traditional privilege log with privilege descriptions.

2. Categorical Privilege Log

A categorical privilege log contains information in specific categories, rather than information pertaining to individual documents. The categories should be reasonably organized and the categorical descriptions should describe the nature of the materials withheld. The number of documents withheld in each category should be detailed along with the names of the attorneys and non-attorneys on the communications.

Plaintiffs v. Defendants
Defendants' Categorical Privilege Log

Category No.	Date Sent Range	Document Types	Sender(s)/ Recipient(s)/ CC(s) of Parent Email	Category Description	Privilege Justification	Number of Documents Withheld (Total Documents)
1	3/13/2024–1/20/2025	Email; Attach; Adobe Acrobat (PDF); Outlook Express Mail Message; Edoc	**Attorneys:** Larry Lawyer (llawyer@lawfirm.com) **Clients:** Debbie Defendant (ddefendant@company.com); Darren Defendant (ddef@company.com); Amy Assistant (aasistant@company.com)	Communications and documents provided to counsel providing, requesting, or reflecting legal advice, or providing information so that legal advice can be given regarding pending litigation	Attorney Client Communication; Attorney Work Product	87
2	9/9/2024–5/1/2025	Email; Attach; Adobe Acrobat (PDF); Outlook Express Mail Message; Microsoft Word 97/98; Microsoft Word 2016; JPEG File Interchange	**Attorneys:** Larry Lawyer (llawyer@lawfirm.com) **Clients:** Debbie Defendant (ddefendant@company.com); Darren Defendant (ddef@company.com); Amy Assistant (aasistant@company.com)	Communications and documents provided to outside counsel providing, requesting, or reflecting legal advice, or providing information so that legal advice can be given regarding pending employee review and termination of Plaintiff	Attorney Client Communication; Attorney Work Product	74

Figure 8.4. Categorical privilege log with category descriptions and number of documents being withheld in that category.

3. Metadata Only Privilege Log

Metadata only privilege logs contain an export of agreed-upon metadata fields without the need to enter separate privilege descriptions for each entry. While this method can save time because there is no need to craft detailed privilege descriptions, some documents may lack sufficient metadata to properly assess a claim of privilege. This missing metadata either can be manually entered to the extent it is available from the face of the document or, if agreed to in an ESI protocol, can remain empty. If enough significant data remains empty, note that a challenge requiring the provision of a more detailed description of the document may be forthcoming.

Plaintiff vs. Defendants
Defendants' Metadata Only Log

No.	Custodian	Email From	Email To	Email CC	Email Subject	Date Sent	File Name	Author	Created	MDS Hash	Privilege Desig-nation	Doc Type
1	Darren Defendant	Darren Defendant (ddef@com-pany.com)	Debbie Defendant (debbiedefed-ant@compa-ny.com); Larry Lawyer (llawyer@law-firm.com)		Documents re: employee termination	1/30/2024	Documents re: employee termination	Darren Defendant	8/5/2025	725C414 D590FED 4C321A7 D8D0669 7BF	Attorney Client Communi-cation	Outlook Express Mail Message
2	Darren Defendant						Employee Evaluation		1/30/2024	D23A7557 BDA8112E 35CC76F D3CD351 80	Attorney Client Communi-cation	Adobe Acrobat (PDF)
3	Debbie Defendant	Debbie Defendant (debbiedefen-dant@com-pany.com)	Darren Defendant (ddef@compa-ny.com); Larry Lawyer (llawyer@law-firm.com)		Question re: next steps for employee termination	3/16/2024	Question re: next steps for employee termination	Debbie Defendant	5/8/2025	723167FC 5CE813F5 F9599318 A5155F4	Attorney Client Communi-cation	Outlook Express Mail Message
4	Debbie Defendant						Employee Evaluation		3/16/2024	0A868D2 BF086532 AE6B3BF 8347874E	Attorney Client Communi-cation	Adobe Acrobat (PDF)
5	Debbie Defendant	Debbie Defendant (debbiedefen-dant@com-pany.com)	Darren Defendant (ddef@compa-ny.com); Larry Lawyer (llawyer@law-firm.com)	Amy Assistant (aasistant @company .com)	Fwd: Potential Settlement Negotiation	3/16/2024	Fwd: Potential Settlement Negotiation	Debbie Defendant	8/5/2025	A974209F 9509ED6 B8F19655 F6AC9BB 4D	Attorney Client Communi-cation	Outlook Express Mail Message
6	Debbie Defendant						Email from Plaintiff		3/16/2024	0A862D2 BF086532 AE6B3BF 8343784E	Attorney Client Communi-cation	Adobe Acrobat (PDF)

Figure 8.5. Metadata only log containing document metadata that was previously agreed upon in the ESI protocol.

D. Using a Review Platform to Export a Log

Manual entry for a privilege log can take a very long time. Luckily, most review platforms offer the ability to export into an Excel spreadsheet any metadata fields that you choose. Additionally, there are often coding layouts that make the addition of privilege descriptions for traditional logs straightforward. It is best to consult with your workspace vendor to discuss efficient ways for extracting data that can be then formatted for a privilege log.

Figure 8.6. Privilege coding layout in a review platform. This layout makes it easy to enter the privilege designation and description and see what metadata will be extracted to accompany these descriptions. Source: Relativity.

Chapter 9

Producing and Receiving the Data

Technical expertise provided by Stephen Johnson

I. Introduction

This chapter will discuss both the form and method of production of data and, conversely, will also discuss how to process data produced by opposing counsel.

II. Steps to Consider before Production

Now that your review is complete and you have identified the relevant, nonprivileged information that should be sent to opposing counsel, there are a few more steps to complete prior to sending your production to opposing counsel via a secure method. When preparing for a production, several steps should be taken to ensure that all responsive documents are produced accurately and efficiently.

A. Create Multiple Search Queries

To best determine whether your potential production set is free of privilege, appropriately tagged for confidentiality, and consistently coded across families, it is helpful to create multiple search queries as a quality control measure. These queries should be tailored to answer the following questions, and the corresponding searches can be created by your review platform vendor.

- Have all documents within my review set been coded with a responsive designation and have any documents with a technical issue or needs further review tag been addressed?
- Are there any documents in which families have coding discrepancies between responsiveness and/or privilege?

- Are there any documents that are tagged as responsive with a privilege designation and are not also redacted, or should those documents be truly withheld?
- Are there any documents requiring redactions and have those redactions been applied to both the document and the metadata?

While this list provides just a few quality control checks that can be completed on a proposed production set, do not hesitate to create additional or tailored searches to ensure that the documents that are to be produced are truly the documents that you want produced.

B. Double Check the Production Set

Now that quality control of the production set has occurred, you are ready to focus on the production itself. Most of these details will have been ironed out in your ESI protocol and will ultimately be handled by your e-discovery vendor. In discussing the production with your e-discovery vendor, consider these questions to ensure the appropriate documents are being produced in the appropriate format:

- Which data set or subset of documents are the focus for production?
- In which format are the documents going to be produced?
- Is there a specific sort order needed or required for your production?
- What Bates prefix and/or number should be applied to the documents?
- Should the Bates numbering be done on a document or page level?
- Which documents should be produced in image format versus native format? (See below for more on this.)
- Have redactions been appropriately applied to images?
- Are there encrypted documents, proprietary file types, or system files that are included and should they have specific placeholders indicating their status to accompany the native document?

C. Prepare the Production and the Export

A vendor will typically handle the next few steps of preparing your production for export; however, it is good to know what goes into this preparation in case questions or issues arise. The typical workflow for preparing a production export is:

- Image all responsive documents that will be produced in TIFF/JPG or PDF formats for any file type that can or should be imaged.
- Run OCR on redacted documents to ensure that redactions are captured in the TEXT/OCR files.

- Configure the export to ensure accuracy of file format and metadata accuracy.
- Preview the metadata, ensure that fields are redacted where appropriate in the presence of redacted images, and review it for potential errors prior to launching the production export.
- Once exported, ensure that all data has been exported in correct file formats, redactions have been captured in both the images and OCR text files, and the correct sort order has been applied.

III. Production Formats

Data is typically produced in two standard forms, and those forms are as follows:

A. PDF Productions

If you are not engaging a review platform vendor, you may choose to simply Bates-stamp and produce PDFs. While not the preferable method of sending or receiving documents, production can be made and ultimately received in PDF format. In fact, if documents have been scanned from paper form or if opposing counsel has requested to receive documents in this format, this is the only available option for processing. As such, when sending or receiving a PDF production, be sure that one PDF is created for each document. Oftentimes, PDFs are produced in one large, often many-thousand-page, document comprised of every document in the production. A production like this often requires unitization from an outside vendor, which adds additional time and cost to the ingestion process. Additionally, if redactions are done on a PDF, be sure that the redaction is burned on to the PDF such that the redaction cannot be easily removed once received by opposing counsel. If you happen to receive documents that are not appropriately redacted, you have an ethical duty to alert opposing counsel of the mistake.[1] Lastly, be aware that a PDF production may pose some challenges for searching due to its lack of metadata.

B. TIFF Productions

The standard form of receiving or producing documents and for loading into a review platform is TIFF images with a load file. In this format, images of the documents are produced, while the load file contains the appropriate metadata fields for each document and the extracted text of each document. For documents that do not image cleanly, such as Excel

1. Model Rule of Professional Conduct 4.4(b).

spreadsheets, natives are often produced in place of an image, and the Bates number is emblazoned on an imaged slipsheet for later reference. Productions in this format are of a better quality and can provide the relevant metadata necessary to conduct advanced searches of the data. In the interest of space and cost savings when using TIFF format, you can configure your imaging profiles in your database/production application for compressed imaging at 300 DPI in black and white or color.

IV. Production of Text Messages and Messaging Application Data

As mentioned previously, for text messages, along with messaging application data such as Teams and Slack, it is important to consider the form of production as well as the time-period that constitutes a "message." Since a message string could go on for days, weeks, or even months, and seemingly extend outside the relevant time period or even the relevant subject matter, explicitly stating what time period should be produced on either side of a relevant message is important. The most common time period utilized is 24 hours.

V. How to Transfer Data Securely

While it may seem easiest to merely zip a folder of documents to send to opposing counsel in a regular email, this method exposes the data to significant risk because general email is not a secure channel for sending data. Additionally, data should never be placed on an open share site. Instead, data transfers should be done through secure FTPs or encrypted hard drives, thumb drives, discs, etc.

Appendix

Sample E-Discovery Documents

The appendixes include sample litigation holds, custodial interview questionnaires, and ESI protocols referenced throughout this book.

Appendix A

Rule 26(f) Memorandum

In the United States District Court
For the Eastern District of Pennsylvania

Plaintiff(s),	**CIVIL ACTION**
v.	**Case No.**
Defendant(s).	

Report of Rule 26(f) Meeting

In accordance with Federal Rule of Civil Procedure 26(f) and this Court's Order Scheduling Hearing, counsel for the parties conferred and submit the following report of their meeting for the court's consideration:

I. <u>Basic Information</u>

Names of counsel for Plaintiff(s) who will participate in the Rule 16 Conference:

Names of counsel for Defendant(s) who will participate in the Rule 16 Conference:

For each party, does counsel have full authority to settle this case at the Rule 16 Conference?

If not, list name(s) of any client or proxy with such authority who will either attend the conference or remain on call during the conference:

Date parties held the Rule 26(f) Conference:

Please check off all that apply:

[ ] Jury Trial Requested [ ] Non-Jury Trial Requested

[ ] Magistrate referral requested [ ] Arbitration

II. Discussion of Claims, Defenses, Relevant Issues, and Likely Motions

Please specify the basis for federal jurisdiction in this case, and discuss whether the parties contest jurisdiction or venue. Briefly summarize the central claims and defenses—you can assume that the court is familiar with the pleadings. Importantly, parties should outline facts and issues necessary to understanding potential motions or discovery issues. **Parties should also attach critical documents to this report for the court to review ahead of the Rule 16 Conference**.

A. Jurisdiction and Venue

Basis of jurisdiction:

Do the parties contest subject matter jurisdiction, personal jurisdiction, or venue?

B. Claims

C. Relief Requested and Amount in Controversy

D. Defenses

E. Amending Pleadings

Do the parties need a deadline to amend pleadings to add claims or additional parties?

If so, propose the earliest practicable filing date.

F. Anticipated Motions

List all threshold motions and dispositive motions that each party has already filed or plans to file. For each motion, specify (1) the applicable Rule that forms the basis for the motion, and (2) summarize the issue.

Proposed timeline for filing dispositive motions:

III. Discovery

A. Informal Disclosure

Will initial disclosures listed in Rule 26(a)(1) be complete before the Rule 16 Conference?

If not, list what is outstanding, and explain why:

Have the parties formed any other agreements as to timing, form, and scope of informal disclosures *not required* in Rule 26(a)(1)?

B. Formal Discovery

The parties anticipate that discovery should be completed within ______ days of the Rule 16 Conference.

If the parties anticipate a discovery period exceeding 90 days past the Rule 16 conference date, please explain why:

Do the parties need to conduct discovery in phases to prepare for the filing of motions or for settlement discussions?

If so, please propose deadlines for phases and what will be due at each phase:

Does either side anticipate the use of experts?

If yes, what is the proposed deadline for expert discovery?[1]

Do the parties expect that they will need to depose any expert witnesses?

Normally, the court expects all expert reports to be submitted simultaneously. If the parties propose to stagger the production of expert reports, please explain why:

Note that Judge Scott expects that the parties will reach an agreement on how to conduct electronic discovery. If the parties cannot reach an agreement before the Rule 16 scheduling conference, the court will enter an order incorporating default standards. The default order can be viewed at Judge Scott's Judge's Info webpage (https://www.paed.uscourts.gov/judges-info/district-court-judges/kai-n-scott). The parties shall discuss the parameters of their anticipated e-discovery at the Rule 26(f) conference, and parties must come to the Rule 16 conference prepared to address e-discovery.

Please identify any other anticipated discovery issues that should be addressed at the Rule 16 Conference, including:

1. Note that Judge Scott's policies and procedures require that parties file all expert reports and CVs at least seven (7) days before a final pretrial conference.

- claims of privilege or of protection as trial-preparation material, as required by Rule 26(f)(3)(D);
- limitations on discovery or protective orders needed; and
- any disputes regarding electronic discovery or agreements regarding electronic discovery that deviate from the court's standard order.

IV. Settlement or Early Resolution

The parties must familiarize themselves with Local Rule 53.3 before responding.

What is the outcome of the parties' discussions about early resolution through alternative dispute resolution (ADR) or mediation?

What is the outcome of the parties' discussions about proceeding before a Magistrate Judge for final disposition?[2]

Is a settlement conference likely to be helpful?

V. Trial Date

A firm date will be scheduled at or shortly after the pre-trial conference. Please either list below or come to the Rule 16 Conference ready with any dates in the three (3) to nine (9) months following the Rule 16 Conference date that present irreversible scheduling conflicts for counsel or the parties. Irreversible scheduling conflicts include pre-paid vacation and planned medical or family leave.

VI. Other Matters

Discuss any other matters not addressed above that parties would like to discuss at the Rule 16 Conference.

____

(Attorney Signature)

____

(Attorney Signature)

2. Magistrate Judges are authorized, with agreement of the parties, to try any civil case, jury or non-jury, with appeals filed directly with the Court of Appeals.

Appendix B

Rule 502(d) Order

502(d) order as printed from the Sedona Conference's Commentary on Protection of Privileged ESI[1]

APPENDIX D: MODEL RULE 502(D) ORDER

[COURT NAME]
[DISTRICT OR COUNTY]

Plaintiff(s),	
vs.	**Case No. ____________**
Defendant(s).	

[PROPOSED] STIPULATED ORDER REGARDING THE DISCLOSURE OF PRIVILEGED INFORMATION

The [insert name of parties], by and through their respective counsel, have jointly stipulated to the terms of Stipulated Order Governing the Disclosure of Privileged Information, and with the Court being fully advised as to the same, it is hereby ORDERED:

I. APPLICABILITY

1. This Order shall be applicable to and govern all deposition transcripts and/or videotapes, and documents produced in response to requests for production of documents, answers to interrogatories, responses to requests for admissions, affidavits, declarations and all other information or material produced, made available for inspection, or otherwise submitted by any of the parties in

1. From The Sedona Conference, *Commentary on the Effective Use of Federal Rule of Evidence 502(d) Orders*, 23 Sedona Conf. J. 1, 50 (2022). Reprinted with permission. For a detailed discussion of applicable law and practice, you may download the entire publication free for individual use at https://thesedonaconference.org/publication/Commentary_on_Effective_Use_of_FRE_502d_Orders.

this litigation as well as testimony adduced at trial or during any hearing (collectively "Information").

II. PRODUCTION OF DISCOVERY MATERIALS CONTAINING POTENTIALLY PRIVILEGED INFORMATION

1. The production of any privileged or otherwise protected or exempted Information, as well as the production of Information without an appropriate designation of confidentiality, shall not be deemed a waiver or impairment of any claim of privilege or protection, including, but not limited to, the attorney-client privilege, the protection afforded to work product materials, or the subject matter thereof, or the confidential nature of any such Information, as to the produced Information, or any other Information.
2. The production of privileged or work-product protected documents, electronically stored information ("ESI") or In formation, whether inadvertent or otherwise, is not a waiver of the privilege or protection from discovery in this case or in any other federal or state proceeding. This Order shall be interpreted to provide the maximum protection allowed by Federal Rule of Evidence 502(d).
3. The producing party must notify the receiving party promptly, in writing, upon discovery that a document has been produced. Upon receiving written notice from the producing party that privileged and/or work-product material has been produced, all such Information, and all copies thereof, shall be returned to the producing party within ten (10) business days of receipt of such notice and the receiving party shall not use such information for any purpose, except as provided in paragraph 5, until further Order of the Court. The receiving party shall also attempt, in good faith, to retrieve and return or destroy all copies of the documents in electronic format.
4. The receiving party may contest the privilege or work-product designation by the producing party, shall give the producing party written notice of the reason for said disagreement. However, the receiving party may not challenge the privilege or immunity claim by arguing that the disclosure itself is a waiver of any applicable privilege. In that instance, the receiving party shall, within fifteen (15) business days from the initial notice by

the producing party, seek an Order from the Court compelling the production of the material.

5. Any analyses, memoranda or notes which were internally generated based upon such produced Information shall immediately be placed in sealed envelopes, and shall be destroyed in the event that (a) the receiving party does not contest that the Information is privileged, or (b) the Court rules that the Information is privileged. Such analyses, memoranda or notes may only be removed from the sealed envelopes and returned to its intended purpose in the event that (a) the producing party agrees in writing that the Information is not privileged, or (b) the Court rules that the Information is not privileged.
6. Nothing contained herein is intended to or shall serve to limit a party's right to conduct a review of documents, ESI or Information (including metadata) for relevance, responsiveness and/or segregation of privileged and/or protected Information before production.

STIPULATED AND AGREED TO on ____________________.

[INSERT NAME OF PLAINTIFF]

By: ______________________________

[INSERT NAME OF DEFENDANT]

By: ______________________________

IT IS SO ORDERED:

____

[Insert name.]
United States District Court Judge

DATED:

Dated: ______________

APPENDIX E: MODEL RULE 502(D) ORDER POSTED BY HON. ANDREW J. PECK (S.D.N.Y.)

UNITED STATES DISTRICT COURT
SOUTHERN DISTRICT OF NEW YORK

________________________________x

RULE 502(d) ORDER

________________________________x

ANDREW J. PECK, United States Magistrate Judge:

1. The production of privileged or work-product protected documents, electronically stored information ("ESI") or information, whether inadvertent or otherwise, is not a waiver of the privilege or protection from discovery in this case or in any other federal or state proceeding. This Order shall be interpreted to provide the maximum protection allowed by Federal Rule of Evidence 502(d).

2. Nothing contained herein is intended to or shall serve to limit a party's right to conduct a review of documents, ESI or information (including metadata) for relevance, responsiveness and/or segregation of privileged and/or protected information before production.

SO ORDERED.

Dated: New York, New York

[DATE]

____

Andrew J. Peck

United States Magistrate Judge

Copies <u>by ECF</u> to: All Counsel
Judge _________________

Appendix C

Confidential Stipulation and Proposed Protective Order

Model Confidentiality Stipulation and Proposed Protective Order from the United States District Court Southern District of New York.

UNITED STATES DISTRICT COURT
SOUTHERN DISTRICT OF NEW YORK

Plaintiff(s), [PLAINTIFF], - *against* - [DEFENDANT]. Defendant(s).	**CONFIDENTIALITY STIPULATION AND PROPOSED PROTECTIVE ORDER** ____ Civ. ____ (____) (AEK)

WHEREAS, the parties having agreed to the following terms of confidentiality, and the Court having found that good cause exists for the issuance of an appropriately tailored confidentiality order pursuant to Rule 26(c) of the Federal Rules of Civil Procedure, it is hereby

ORDERED that the following restrictions and procedures shall apply to the information and documents exchanged by the parties in connection with the pre-trial phase of this action:

1. Counsel for any party may designate any document or information, in whole or in part, as confidential if counsel determines, in good faith, that such designation is necessary to protect the interests of the client in information that is proprietary, a trade secret, or otherwise sensitive non-public information ("Confidential Information"). Information and documents designated by a party as confidential will be stamped "CONFIDENTIAL."

2. The Confidential Information disclosed will be held and used by the person receiving such information solely for use in connection with the action.

3. In the event a party challenges another party's designation of confidentiality, counsel shall make a good faith effort to resolve the dispute, and in the absence of a resolution, the challenging party may seek resolution by the Court. Nothing in this Protective Order constitutes an admission by any party that Confidential Information disclosed in this case is relevant or admissible. Each party reserves the right to object to the use or admissibility of the Confidential Information.

4. Documents designated as "CONFIDENTIAL" shall not be disclosed to any person, except:

a. The requesting party and counsel, including in-house counsel;

b. Employees of such counsel assigned to and necessary to assist in the litigation;

c. Consultants or experts assisting in the prosecution or defense of the matter, to the extent deemed necessary by counsel; and

d. The Court (including the mediator, or other person having access to any Confidential Information by virtue of his or her position with the Court).

The parties should meet and confer if any production requires a designation of "For Attorneys' or Experts' Eyes Only."

5. Prior to disclosing or displaying the Confidential Information to any person, counsel must:

a. Inform the person of the confidential nature of the information or documents;

b. Inform the person that this Court has enjoined the use of the information or documents by him/her for any purpose other than this litigation and has enjoined the disclosure of the information or documents to any other person; and

c. Require each such person to sign an agreement to be bound by this Order in the form attached as Exhibit A.

6. The disclosure of a document or information without designating it as "CONFIDENTIAL" shall not constitute a waiver of the right to designate such document or information as Confidential Information. If so designated, the document or information shall thereafter be treated as Confidential Information subject to all the terms of this Stipulation and Order.

7. Any Personally Identifying Information ("PII") (e.g., social security numbers, financial account numbers, passwords, and information that may be used for identity theft) exchanged in discovery shall be maintained by the receiving party in a manner that is secure.

8. Pursuant to Federal Rule of Evidence 502, the production of privileged or work product protected documents or communications, electronically stored information ("ESI") or information, whether inadvertent or otherwise, shall not constitute a waiver of the privilege or protection from discovery in this case or in any other federal or state proceeding. This Order shall be interpreted to provide the maximum protection allowed by Federal Rule of Evidence 502(d). Nothing contained herein is intended to or shall serve to limit a party's right to conduct a review of documents, ESI or information (including metadata) for relevance, responsiveness and/or segregation of privileged and/or protected information before production.

9. Notwithstanding the designation of information as "CONFIDENTIAL" in discovery, there is no presumption that such information shall be filed with the Court under seal. The parties shall follow the Court's procedures for requests for filing under seal.

10. At the conclusion of litigation, Confidential Information and any copies thereof shall be promptly (and in no event later than 30 days after entry of final judgment no longer subject to further appeal) returned to the producing party or certified as destroyed, except that the parties' counsel shall be permitted to retain their working files on the condition that those files will remain protected.

11. Nothing herein shall preclude the parties from disclosing material designated to be Confidential Information if otherwise required by law or pursuant to a valid subpoena.

SO STIPULATED AND AGREED.

Dated: _________, 20___
White Plains, New York

_________________________ _________________________
Counsel for Plaintiff(s) Counsel for Defendant(s)

SO ORDERED.

____
United States Magistrate Judge

EXHIBIT A

Agreement

I have been informed by counsel that certain documents or information to be disclosed to me in connection with the matter entitled ________________________ have been designated as confidential. I have been informed that any such documents or information labeled "CONFIDENTIAL" are confidential by Order of the Court. I hereby agree that I will not disclose any information contained in such documents to any other person. I further agree not to use any such information for any purpose other than this litigation.

Dated: __________, 20___

__________________________ __________________________

Name (printed) Signature

Signed in the presence of:

____

(Attorney)

Appendix D

Model Confidentiality Order

Model Confidentiality Order for the United States District Court for the Northern District of Illinois

Form LR 26.2
MODEL CONFIDENTIALITY ORDER

UNITED STATES DISTRICT COURT
NORTHERN DISTRICT OF ILLINOIS

Plaintiff	)	
v.	)	Civil No.
	)	District Judge
	)	Magistrate Judge
Defendant	)	

[Agreed][1] Confidentiality Order

[If by agreement] The parties to this Agreed Confidentiality Order have agreed to the terms of this Order; accordingly, it is ORDERED:

[If not fully agreed] A party to this action has moved that the Court enter a confidentiality order. The Court has determined that the terms set forth herein are appropriate to protect the respective interests of the parties, the public, and the Court. Accordingly, it is ORDERED:

1. **Scope.** All materials produced or adduced in the course of discovery, including initial disclosures, responses to discovery requests, deposition testimony and exhibits, and information derived directly therefrom (hereinafter collectively

---

1 Counsel should include or delete language in brackets as necessary to the specific case. **Any other changes to this model order must be shown by redlining that indicates both deletions and additions to the model text.** Counsel may also modify this model order as appropriate for the circumstances of the case. This model order is for the convenience of the parties and the court and not intended to create a presumption in favor of the provisions in this model order and against alternative language proposed by the parties. The court will make the final decision on the terms of any order notwithstanding the agreement of the parties.

"documents"), shall be subject to this Order concerning Confidential Information as defined below. This Order is subject to the Local Rules of this District and the Federal Rules of Civil Procedure on matters of procedure and calculation of time periods.

2. **Confidential Information.** As used in this Order, "Confidential Information" means information designated as "CONFIDENTIAL-SUBJECT TO PROTECTIVE ORDER" by the producing party that falls within one or more of the following categories: (a) information prohibited from disclosure by statute; (b) information that reveals trade secrets; (c) research, technical, commercial or financial information that the party has maintained as confidential; (d) medical information concerning any individual; (e) personal identity information; (f) income tax returns (including attached schedules and forms), W-2 forms and 1099 forms; or (g) personnel or employment records of a person who is not a party to the case.[2] Information or documents that are available to the public may not be designated as Confidential Information.

3. **Designation.**

(a) A party may designate a document as Confidential Information for protection under this Order by placing or affixing the words "CONFIDENTIAL - SUBJECT TO PROTECTIVE ORDER" on the document and on all copies in a manner that will not interfere with the legibility of the document. As used in this Order, "copies" includes electronic images, duplicates, extracts, summaries or descriptions that contain

2 If protection is sought for any other category of information, the additional category shall be described in paragraph 2 with the additional language redlined to show the change in the proposed Order.

the Confidential Information. The marking "CONFIDENTIAL - SUBJECT TO PROTECTIVE ORDER" shall be applied prior to or at the time of the documents are produced or disclosed. Applying the marking "CONFIDENTIAL - SUBJECT TO PROTECTIVE ORDER" to a document does not mean that the document has any status or protection by statute or otherwise except to the extent and for the purposes of this Order. Any copies that are made of any documents marked "CONFIDENTIAL - SUBJECT TO PROTECTIVE ORDER" shall also be so marked, except that indices, electronic databases or lists of documents that do not contain substantial portions or images of the text of marked documents and do not otherwise disclose the substance of the Confidential Information are not required to be marked.

(b) The designation of a document as Confidential Information is a certification by an attorney or a party appearing *pro se* that the document contains Confidential Information as defined in this order.[3]

4. Depositions.[4]

Alternative A. Deposition testimony is protected by this Order only if designated as "CONFIDENTIAL – SUBJECT TO PROTECTIVE ORDER" on the record at the time the testimony is taken. Such designation shall be specific as to the portions that contain

---

3 An attorney who reviews the documents and designates them as CONFIDENTIAL - SUBJECT TO PROTECTIVE ORDER must be admitted to the Bar of at least one state but need not be admitted to practice in the Northern District of Illinois unless the lawyer is appearing generally in the case on behalf of a party. By designating documents confidential pursuant to this Order, counsel submits to the jurisdiction and sanctions of this Court on the subject matter of the designation.

4 The parties or movant seeking the order shall select one alternative for handling deposition testimony and delete by redlining the alternative provision that is not chosen.

Confidential Information. Deposition testimony so designated shall be treated as Confidential Information protected by this Order until fourteen days after delivery of the transcript by the court reporter to any party or the witness. Within fourteen days after delivery of the transcript, a designating party may serve a Notice of Designation to all parties of record identifying the specific portions of the transcript that are designated Confidential Information, and thereafter those portions identified in the Notice of Designation shall be protected under the terms of this Order. The failure to serve a timely Notice of Designation waives any designation of deposition testimony as Confidential Information that was made on the record of the deposition, unless otherwise ordered by the Court.

Alternative B. Unless all parties agree on the record at the time the deposition testimony is taken, all deposition testimony taken in this case shall be treated as Confidential Information until the expiration of the following: No later than the fourteenth day after the transcript is delivered to any party or the witness, and in no event later than 60 days after the testimony was given, Within this time period, a party may serve a Notice of Designation to all parties of record as to specific portions of the testimony that are designated Confidential Information, and thereafter only those portions identified in the Notice of Designation shall be protected by the terms of this Order. The failure to serve a timely Notice of Designation shall waive any designation of testimony taken in that deposition as Confidential Information, unless otherwise ordered by the Court.

5. Protection of Confidential Material.

(a) General Protections. Confidential Information shall not be used or disclosed by the parties, counsel for the parties or any other persons identified in subparagraph (b) for any purpose whatsoever other than in this litigation, including any appeal thereof. **[INCLUDE IN PUTATIVE CLASS ACTION CASE:** In a putative class action, Confidential Information may be disclosed only to the named plaintiff(s) and not to any other member of the putative class unless and until a class including the putative member has been certified.]

(b) Limited Third-Party Disclosures. The parties and counsel for the parties shall not disclose or permit the disclosure of any Confidential Information to any third person or entity except as set forth in subparagraphs (1)-(9). Subject to these requirements, the following categories of persons may be allowed to review Confidential Information:

(1) **Counsel.** Counsel for the parties and employees of counsel who have responsibility for the action;

(2) **Parties.** Individual parties and employees of a party but only to the extent counsel determines in good faith that the employee's assistance is reasonably necessary to the conduct of the litigation in which the information is disclosed;

(3) **The Court and its personnel;**

(4) **Court Reporters and Recorders.** Court reporters and recorders engaged for depositions;

(5) **Contractors.** Those persons specifically engaged for the limited purpose of making copies of documents or organizing or processing documents, including outside vendors hired to process electronically stored documents;

(6) **Consultants and Experts**. Consultants, investigators, or experts employed by the parties or counsel for the parties to assist in the preparation and trial of this action but only after such persons have completed the certification contained in Attachment A, Acknowledgment of Understanding and Agreement to Be Bound;

(7) **Witnesses at depositions**. During their depositions, witnesses in this action to whom disclosure is reasonably necessary. Witnesses shall not retain a copy of documents containing Confidential Information, except witnesses may receive a copy of all exhibits marked at their depositions in connection with review of the transcripts. Pages of transcribed deposition testimony or exhibits to depositions that are designated as Confidential Information pursuant to the process set out in this Order must be separately bound by the court reporter and may not be disclosed to anyone except as permitted under this Order.

(8) **Author or recipient.** The author or recipient of the document (not including a person who received the document in the course of litigation); and

(9) Others by Consent. Other persons only by written consent of the producing party or upon order of the Court and on such conditions as may be agreed or ordered.

(c) **Control of Documents**. Counsel for the parties shall make reasonable efforts to prevent unauthorized or inadvertent disclosure of Confidential Information. Counsel shall maintain the originals of the forms signed by persons acknowledging their obligations under this Order for a period of three years after the termination of the case.

6. **Inadvertent Failure to Designate.** An inadvertent failure to designate a document as Confidential Information does not, standing alone, waive the right to so designate the document; provided, however, that a failure to serve a timely Notice of Designation of deposition testimony as required by this Order, even if inadvertent, waives any protection for deposition testimony. If a party designates a document as

Confidential Information after it was initially produced, the receiving party, on notification of the designation, must make a reasonable effort to assure that the document is treated in accordance with the provisions of this Order. No party shall be found to have violated this Order for failing to maintain the confidentiality of material during a time when that material has not been designated Confidential Information, even where the failure to so designate was inadvertent and where the material is subsequently designated Confidential Information.

7. **Filing of Confidential Information.** This Order does not, by itself, authorize the filing of any document under seal. Any party wishing to file a document designated as Confidential Information in connection with a motion, brief or other submission to the Court must comply with LR 26.2.

8. **No Greater Protection of Specific Documents.** Except on privilege grounds not addressed by this Order, no party may withhold information from discovery on the ground that it requires protection greater than that afforded by this Order unless the party moves for an order providing such special protection.

9. **Challenges by a Party to Designation as Confidential Information.** The designation of any material or document as Confidential Information is subject to challenge by any party. The following procedure shall apply to any such challenge.

(a) **Meet and Confer.** A party challenging the designation of Confidential Information must do so in good faith and must begin the process by conferring directly with counsel for the designating party. In conferring, the challenging party must explain the basis for its belief that the confidentiality designation was not proper and must give the designating party an opportunity to review the designated material, to reconsider the designation, and, if no change in designation is offered, to explain the basis for the designation. The designating party must respond to the challenge within five (5) business days.

(b) Judicial Intervention. A party that elects to challenge a confidentiality designation may file and serve a motion that identifies the challenged material and sets forth in detail the basis for the challenge. Each such motion must be accompanied by a competent declaration that affirms that the movant has complied with the meet and confer requirements of this procedure. The burden of persuasion in any such challenge proceeding shall be on the designating party. Until the Court rules on the challenge, all parties shall continue to treat the materials as Confidential Information under the terms of this Order.

10. Action by the Court. Applications to the Court for an order relating to materials or documents designated Confidential Information shall be by motion. Nothing in this Order or any action or agreement of a party under this Order limits the Court's power to make orders concerning the disclosure of documents produced in discovery or at trial.

11. Use of Confidential Documents or Information at Trial. Nothing in this Order shall be construed to affect the use of any document, material, or information at any trial or hearing. A party that intends to present or that anticipates that another party may present Confidential information at a hearing or trial shall bring that issue to the Court's and parties' attention by motion or in a pretrial memorandum without disclosing the Confidential Information. The Court may thereafter make such orders as are necessary to govern the use of such documents or information at trial.

12. Confidential Information Subpoenaed or Ordered Produced in Other Litigation.

(a) If a receiving party is served with a subpoena or an order issued in other litigation that would compel disclosure of any material or document designated in this action as Confidential Information, the receiving party must so notify the designating party, in writing, immediately and in no event more than three court days after receiving the subpoena or order. Such notification must include a copy of the subpoena or court order.

(b) The receiving party also must immediately inform in writing the party who caused the subpoena or order to issue in the other litigation that some or all of the material covered by the subpoena or order is the subject of this Order. In addition, the receiving party must deliver a copy of this Order promptly to the party in the other action that caused the subpoena to issue.

(c) The purpose of imposing these duties is to alert the interested persons to the existence of this Order and to afford the designating party in this case an opportunity to try to protect its Confidential Information in the court from which the subpoena or order issued. The designating party shall bear the burden and the expense of seeking protection in that court of its Confidential Information, and nothing in these provisions should be construed as authorizing or encouraging a receiving party in this action to disobey a lawful directive from another court. The obligations set forth in this paragraph remain in effect while the party has in its possession, custody or control Confidential Information by the other party to this case.

13. Challenges by Members of the Public to Sealing Orders. A party or interested member of the public has a right to challenge the sealing of particular documents that have been filed under seal, and the party asserting confidentiality will have the burden of demonstrating the propriety of filing under seal.

14. Obligations on Conclusion of Litigation.

(a) Order Continues in Force. Unless otherwise agreed or ordered, this Order shall remain in force after dismissal or entry of final judgment not subject to further appeal.

(b) Obligations at Conclusion of Litigation. Within sixty-three days after dismissal or entry of final judgment not subject to further appeal, all Confidential Information and documents marked "CONFIDENTIAL - SUBJECT TO PROTECTIVE ORDER" under this Order, including copies as defined in ¶ 3(a), shall be returned to the producing party unless: (1) the document has been offered into evidence or filed without restriction as to disclosure; (2) the parties agree to destruction to the extent practicable in lieu of return;[5] or (3) as to documents bearing the notations, summations, or other mental impressions of the receiving party, that party elects to destroy the documents and certifies to the producing party that it has done so.

---

5 The parties may choose to agree that the receiving party shall destroy documents containing Confidential Information and certify the fact of destruction, and that the receiving party shall not be required to locate, isolate and return e-mails (including attachments to e-mails) that may include Confidential Information, or Confidential Information contained in deposition transcripts or drafts or final expert reports.

(c) Retention of Work Product and one set of Filed Documents. Notwithstanding the above requirements to return or destroy documents, counsel may retain (1) attorney work product, including an index that refers or relates to designated Confidential Information so long as that work product does not duplicate verbatim substantial portions of Confidential Information, and (2) one complete set of all documents filed with the Court including those filed under seal. Any retained Confidential Information shall continue to be protected under this Order. An attorney may use his or her work product in subsequent litigation, provided that its use does not disclose or use Confidential Information.

(d) Deletion of Documents filed under Seal from Electronic Case Filing (ECF) System. Filings under seal shall be deleted from the ECF system only upon order of the Court.

15. Order Subject to Modification. This Order shall be subject to modification by the Court on its own initiative or on motion of a party or any other person with standing concerning the subject matter.

16. No Prior Judicial Determination. This Order is entered based on the representations and agreements of the parties and for the purpose of facilitating discovery. Nothing herein shall be construed or presented as a judicial determination that any document or material designated Confidential Information by counsel or the parties is entitled to protection under Rule 26(c) of the Federal Rules of Civil Procedure or otherwise until such time as the Court may rule on a specific document or issue.

17. **Persons Bound.** This Order shall take effect when entered and shall be binding upon all counsel of record and their law firms, the parties, and persons made subject to this Order by its terms.

So Ordered.

Dated: ______________________________

U.S. District Judge
U.S. Magistrate Judge

[Delete signature blocks if not wholly by agreement]

WE SO MOVE
and agree to abide by the terms of this Order

____
Signature

____
Printed Name

Counsel for: ____________________

Dated:

WE SO MOVE
and agree to abide by the terms of this Order

____
Signature

____
Printed Name

Counsel for: ____________________

Dated:

ATTACHMENT A

UNITED STATES DISTRICT COURT
NORTHERN DISTRICT OF ILLINOIS

	)	
	)	Civil No.
Plaintiff	)	
	)	
	)	
	)	
Defendant	)	

ACKNOWLEDGMENT
AND
AGREEMENT TO BE BOUND

The undersigned hereby acknowledges that he/she has read the Confidentiality Order dated ______________________________ in the above-captioned action and attached hereto, understands the terms thereof, and agrees to be bound by its terms. The undersigned submits to the jurisdiction of the United States District Court for the Northern District of Illinois in matters relating to the Confidentiality Order and understands that the terms of the Confidentiality Order obligate him/her to use materials designated as Confidential Information in accordance with the Order solely for the purposes of the above-captioned action, and not to disclose any such Confidential Information to any other person, firm or concern.

The undersigned acknowledges that violation of the Confidentiality Order may result in penalties for contempt of court.

Name: ______________________________

Job Title: ______________________________

Employer: ______________________________

Business Address: ______________________

____

____

Date: ______________ ______________________

Signature

Adopted 06/29/12

Appendix E

Comprehensive ESI Protocol

UNITED STATES DISTRICT COURT

IN RE ________________________ This Document Relates To: All Actions	Case No. _______________ **ORDER REGARDING PRODUCTION OF ELECTRONICALLY STORED INFORMATION AND PAPER DOCUMENTS**

This Order Regarding Production Of Electronically Stored Information And Paper Documents ("ESI Protocol Order") shall govern the Parties in the above-captioned case whether they currently are involved or become so in the future, and any related actions that may later be consolidated with this case (collectively, the "Litigation").

Nothing in this ESI Protocol Order shall be construed to affect the admissibility of discoverable information. Pursuant to the terms of this ESI Protocol Order, information regarding search process and electronically-stored information ("ESI") practices may be disclosed, but compliance with this ESI Protocol Order does not constitute a waiver, by any Party, of any objection to the production of particular ESI as irrelevant, undiscoverable, or otherwise inadmissible, unduly burdensome or not reasonably accessible, or privileged, nor does it constitute a waiver of any right to discovery by any Party. For the avoidance of doubt, a Party's compliance with this ESI Protocol Order will not be interpreted to require disclosure of information potentially protected by the attorney-client privilege, the work product doctrine, or any other applicable privilege.

I. GENERAL PROVISIONS

A. **Applicability:** This ESI Protocol Order will govern the production of ESI and paper documents. To the extent that a Party collected and processed documents prior to the entry of this ESI Protocol Order, and production of such documents cannot be made in accordance with the terms of this ESI Protocol Order, the Parties will meet and confer concerning the potential formats of the production of any such documents.

B. **Cooperation:** The Parties agree that they will adhere to the principles of cooperation, transparency, reasonableness, and proportionality, as set forth in the Federal Rules of Civil Procedure and as interpreted by federal case law and in the Seventh Circuit Electronic Discovery Committee Principles Relating to the Discovery of Electronically Stored Information, as they conduct discovery in the Litigation.

C. **ESI Liaisons:**

1. **Designation:** Each Party agrees to designate an ESI Liaison within 7 days after entry of this ESI Protocol Order. Any Party is free to change its designated ESI Liaison by providing written notice to the other Parties.

2. **Duties of ESI Liaison:** Each ESI Liaison will be prepared to participate in the resolution of any e-discovery disputes or ESI issues that may arise (or designate another person as primarily responsible) and have access to personnel most knowledgeable about the Party's electronic systems and capabilities in order to, as appropriate, answer pertinent questions.

3. **Time Frame for ESI Issue Resolution:** Each ESI Liaison will acknowledge receipt of an ESI-related inquiry from another ESI Liaison within 3 business days after the initial inquiry and respond substantively no later than 10 business days after the initial inquiry. If the responding

ESI Liaison believes the ESI issue in question is particularly complex and requires more than 10 business days to respond substantively, then within 10 business days the responding ESI Liaison will provide a general explanation of the process necessary to answer the question and provide an estimated response date.

D. **Deadlines**. References to schedules and deadlines in this ESI Protocol Order shall comply with Fed. R. Civ. P. 6 with respect to computing deadlines.

E. **Definitions:**

1. "Discovery Material" is defined as all information produced, given, or exchanged by and among all Parties, or received from non-Parties in the Litigation, including all deposition testimony, testimony given at hearings or other proceedings, interrogatory answers, documents and all other discovery materials, whether produced informally or in response to requests for discovery.

2. Plaintiffs and Defendants, as well as their officers, directors, employees, agents, and legal counsel, are referred to as the "Parties" solely for the purposes of this ESI Protocol Order. A single Plaintiff or Defendant, as well as, where applicable, its respective officers, directors, employees, agents, and legal counsel, may also be referred to as a "Party" solely for the purposes of this ESI Protocol Order.

3. "Plaintiffs" as used herein shall mean the putative Direct Purchaser Plaintiff class, Commercial and Institutional Indirect Purchaser Plaintiff class, and End-User Consumer Plaintiff class as set forth in the respective operative complaints.

4. "Defendants" as used herein shall mean Defendants.

5. To avoid misunderstandings about terms, all Parties should consult the most current edition of The Sedona Conference Glossary.

F. **Authenticity and Admissibility:** Nothing in this ESI Protocol Order shall be construed to affect the authenticity or admissibility of any document or data. All objections to the authenticity or admissibility of any document or data are preserved and may be asserted at any time.

G. **Confidential Information:** For the avoidance of doubt, nothing herein shall contradict the Parties' rights and obligations with respect to any information designated as confidential under the Agreed Confidentiality Order (Dkt. 202).

H. **Encryption:** To maximize the security of information in transit, any media on which documents are produced may be encrypted by the producing Party. In such cases, the producing Party shall transmit the encryption key or password to the requesting Party, under separate cover, contemporaneously with sending the encrypted media.

II. GENERAL PRODUCTION FORMAT PROTOCOLS

A. **TIFFs:** Except for structured data, all production images will be provided as a black-and-white, single-page Group IV TIFF of at least 300 DPI resolution with corresponding multi-page text and necessary load files. Each image will have a file name that is the unique Bates number of that image, pursuant to ¶ II(E). Original document orientation should be maintained to the extent reasonably practicable and technologically possible for a producing Party's vendor (i.e., portrait to portrait and landscape to landscape). Hidden content, tracked changes, edits, comments, notes, and other similar information viewable within the native file shall, to the extent reasonably practicable, also be imaged so that this information is captured on the produced image file. Documents that are difficult to render in TIFF because of technical issues, or any other documents that are impracticable to render in TIFF format, may be produced in their native format with a placeholder TIFF image stating "Document Produced Natively," unless such documents contain redactions, in which case the documents will be produced in TIFF format. A producing Party retains the option to produce ESI in alternative formats if so agreed by the requesting Party, which may include native format, or a combination of native and TIFF formats.

B. **Text Files:** Each ESI item produced under this ESI Protocol Order shall be accompanied by a text file as set out below. All text files shall be provided as a single document level text file for each item, not one text file per page. Each text file shall be named to use the Bates number of the first page of the corresponding production item.

1. **OCR:** A producing Party may make paper documents available for inspection and copying/scanning in accordance with FED. R. CIV. P. 34 or, additionally or alternatively, scan and OCR paper documents if it chooses. Where OCR is used, the Parties will endeavor to generate accurate OCR and will utilize quality OCR processes and technology. OCR text files should indicate page breaks where possible. Even if OCR is used by a producing Party, however, the Parties acknowledge that, due to poor quality of the originals, not all documents lend themselves to the generation of accurate OCR. In such instances, or in the event that a producing Party does not choose to use OCR at all, the producing Party will make the paper documents available for inspection and copying in accordance with FED. R. CIV. P. 34.

2. **ESI:** Emails and other ESI will be accompanied by extracted text taken from the electronic file itself, where available

C. **Production of Native Items:** The Parties agree that ESI shall be produced as TIFFs with an accompanying load file, which will contain, among other data points, the ESI data points listed in Appendix 1 hereto. The exception to this rule shall be spreadsheet-application files (e.g., MS Excel), personal databases (e.g., MS Access), and multimedia audio/visual files such as voice and video recordings (e.g., .wav, .mpeg, and .avi), for which all ESI items shall be produced in native format upon reasonable request. In the case of personal database (e.g., MS Access) files containing confidential or privileged information, the Parties shall meet and confer to determine the appropriate form of production. In addition to producing the above file types in native format, the producing Party shall produce a single-page TIFF slip sheet indicating that a native item was produced. The corresponding load file shall include NativeFileLink information for each native file that is produced. Further, the Parties agree to meet and confer prior to producing native file types other than MS Excel and multimedia audio/visual file types such as .wav, .mpeg and .avi. Prior to processing non-standard native files for production, the producing Party shall disclose the file type to and meet and confer with the requesting Party on a reasonably useable production format. The Parties agree to meet and confer to the extent that there is data in database application files, such as SQL and SAP, to determine the best reasonable form of production of usable data. Through the pendency of the Litigation, the producing Party shall exercise reasonable, good faith efforts to maintain all preserved and produced native files in a manner that does not materially alter or modify the file or the metadata.

D. **Requests for Other Native Files:** Other than as specifically set forth above, a producing Party need not produce documents in native format. If a Party would like a particular document produced in native format and this ESI Protocol Order does not require the production of that document in its native format, the Party making such a request shall explain the reason for its request that the document be produced in its native format. The requesting Party will provide a specific Bates range for documents it wishes to be produced in native format. Any native files that are produced should be produced with a link in the NativeLink field, along with all extracted text and applicable metadata fields set forth in Appendix 1.

E. **Bates Numbering:**

1. All images must be assigned a Bates number that must always: (1) be unique across the entire document production; (2) maintain a constant prefix and length (ten-digits and 0-padded) across the entire production; (3) contain no special characters or embedded spaces, except hyphens or underscores; (4) be sequential within a given document; and (5) identify the producing Party. To the extent reasonably practicable, the Bates number must also maintain consistent numbering across a family of documents.

2. If a Bates number or set of Bates numbers is skipped in a production, the producing Party will so note in a cover letter or production log accompanying the production.

3. The producing Party will brand all TIFF images at a location that does not obliterate or obscure any part of the underlying images.

F. **Parent-Child Relationships:** Parent-child relationships (the association between an attachment and its parent document) that have been maintained in the ordinary course of business should be preserved to the extent reasonably practicable. For example, if a Party is producing a hard copy printout of an email with its attachments, the attachments should be processed in order behind the e-mail to the extent reasonably practicable.

G. **Non-Responsive Attachments:** The Parties agree that non-responsive parent documents must be produced if they contain a responsive attachment and are not withheld as privileged. Non-responsive attachments to responsive parent emails need not be produced, but the Parties will meet and confer regarding a non-exhaustive list of criteria in determining whether a document is responsive within the meaning of Rule 26(b)(1) for purposes of the Litigation. The list may be specific to each Party. A Bates numbered placeholder will be provided for any document withheld pursuant to this ¶ II(G) and shall state that a non-responsive attachment has been withheld from production. The Parties will meet and confer regarding whether any other information will be contained on the placeholder to describe the category of document withheld by a producing Party. The requesting Party has the right to request the production of any attachment withheld solely on the basis of non-responsiveness that the requesting Party believes in good faith is responsive. For such attachments, the requesting Party shall provide a list of Bates numbers of any document produced that suggests that a responsive attachment was excluded from production as a non-responsive attachment and of any such attachment the requesting Party seeks to have produced, as well as explain why it believes the attachment is responsive.

H. **Load Files:** All production items will be provided with a delimited data file or "load file," which will include both an image cross-reference load file (such as an Opticon file) as well as a metadata (.dat) file with the metadata fields identified below on the document level to the extent available. The load file must reference each TIFF in the corresponding production. The total number of documents referenced in a production's data load file should match the total number of designated document breaks in the Image Load files in the production.

I. **Color:** Documents or ESI containing color need not be produced initially in color. However, if an original document or ESI item contains color markings and it is necessary to see those markings in their original color to understand the meaning or content of the document, then the requesting Party may, in good faith, request that the document or ESI item be produced in its original colors. For such documents, the requesting Party shall provide a list of Bates numbers of the imaged documents sought to be produced in color. The production of documents and/or ESI in color shall be made in single-page JPEG format (300 DPI). All requirements for productions stated in this ESI Protocol Order regarding productions in TIFF format apply to any productions of documents and/or ESI in color made in such an alternative format. Requests that a document be produced in color for the reasons set forth in this ¶ II(I) will not be unreasonably denied by the producing Party. If a producing Party wishes to object, it may do so by responding in writing and setting forth its objection(s) to the production of the requested document in color.

J. **Confidentiality Designations:** If a particular paper document or ESI item qualifies for confidential treatment pursuant to any applicable federal, state, or common law (e.g., Personally Identifiable Information or Protected Health Information), or to the terms of a Protective Order entered by the Court in the Litigation or a confidentiality stipulation entered into by the Parties, the designation shall be branded on the document's image at a location that does not obliterate or obscure any part of the underlying images. To the extent reasonably possible, this designation also should be included in the appropriate data field in the load file. Failure to comply with the procedures set forth in this ESI Protocol Order, any protective order or confidential order, or any confidential stipulation shall not waive any protection or confidential treatment.

K. **Production Media & Protocol:** A producing Party may produce documents via email or via file-sharing service, including any network-based secure file transfer mechanism or FTP protocol. Any requesting Party that is unable to resolve any technical issues with the electronic production method used for a particular production may request that a producing Party provide a copy of that production using Production Media, as described below in this ¶ II(K).

A producing Party may also produce documents on readily accessible computer or electronic media, including CD-ROM, DVD, or external hard drive (with standard PC compatible interface) ("Production Media"). All Production Media will be encrypted, and the producing Party will provide a decryption key to the requesting Party in a communication separate from the production itself. Each piece of Production Media will be assigned a production number or other unique identifying label corresponding to the date of the production of documents on the Production Media, as well as the sequence of the material in that production. For example, if the production comprises document images on three DVDs, the producing Party may label each DVD in the following manner: "[PARTY] Production January 1, 2017-001," "[PARTY] Production January 1, 2017-002," and "[PARTY] Production January 1, 2017-003." Where the Production Media used is a CD-ROM, DVD, external hard drive (with standard PC compatible interface), or USB drive, such production media must be sent no slower than overnight delivery via FedEx, UPS, or USPS. Each item of Production Media (or in the case of productions made via FTP link, each production transmittal letter) shall include: (1) text referencing that it was produced in [redacted], (2) the production date, (3) the Bates number range of the materials contained on such production media item, and (4) a short description of the production. Any replacement Production Media will cross-reference the original Production Media and clearly identify that it is a replacement and cross-reference the Bates number range that is being replaced. The ESI Liaisons shall designate the appropriate physical address for productions that are produced on Production Media.

However produced, a producing Party shall provide clear instructions for accessing the production, including any necessary passwords or encryption keys.

III. PAPER DOCUMENT PRODUCTION PROTOCOLS

A. **Scanning:** A producing Party may make paper documents available for inspection and copying in accordance with FED. R. CIV. P. 34 or, additionally or alternatively, OCR paper documents if it chooses. Where OCR is used, the Parties agree that the following ¶¶ III(B)-(E) shall apply.

B. **Coding Fields:** The following information shall be produced in the load file accompanying production of paper documents: (a) BegBates, (b) EndBates, (c) BegAttach, (d) EndAttach, (e) Custodian, (f) Confidentiality, and (g) Redacted (Y/N). Additionally, all paper documents will be produced with a coding field named "Paper Document" marked with a "Y."

C. **Unitization of Paper Documents:** Paper documents should be logically unitized for production to the extent reasonably practicable. Therefore, when scanning paper documents for production, distinct documents shall not be merged into a single record and single documents shall not be split into multiple records.

D. **File/Binder Structures:**

1. **Unitization:** Where the documents were organized into groups, such as folders, clipped bundles, and binders, this structure shall be maintained and provided in the load file to the extent reasonably practicable. The relationship among the documents in a folder or other grouping should be reflected in proper coding of the beginning and ending document and attachment fields to the extent reasonably practicable. The Parties will make their best efforts to unitize documents correctly.

2. **Identification:** Where a document, or a document group – such as folder, clipped bundle, or binder – has an identification spine or other label, the information on the label shall be scanned and produced as the first page of the document or grouping.

E. **Custodian Identification:** The Parties will utilize best efforts to ensure that paper records for a particular Document Custodian are produced in consecutive Bates stamp order. *See infra* ¶ V(B)(1).

IV. ESI METADATA FORMAT AND PROCESSING ISSUES

A. **System Files:** ESI productions may be de-NISTed using the industry standard list of such files maintained in the National Software Reference Library by the National Institute of Standards & Technology as it exists at the time of de-

NISTing. Other file types may be added to the list of excluded files by agreement of the Parties.

B. **Metadata Fields and Processing:**

1. **Date and Time:** No Party shall modify the date or time as contained in any original ESI.

2. **Time Zone:** To the extent reasonably practicable, ESI items shall be processed using a consistent time zone (e.g., GMT), and the time zone used shall be disclosed to the requesting Party.

3. **Auto Date/Time Stamps:** To the extent reasonably practicable, ESI items shall be processed so as to preserve the date/time shown in the document as it was last saved, not the date of collection or processing.

4. Except as otherwise set forth in this ESI Protocol Order, ESI files shall be produced with at least each of the data fields set forth in Appendix 1 that can reasonably be extracted from a document.

5. The Parties are not obligated to manually populate any of the fields in Appendix 1 if such fields cannot reasonably be extracted from the document using an automated process, with the exception of the following fields: (a) BegBates, (b) EndBates, (c) BegAttach, (d) EndAttach, (e) Custodian, (f) Confidentiality, (g) Redacted (Y/N), and (h) NativeLink fields, which should be populated regardless of whether the fields can be populated pursuant to an automated process.

C. **Redaction:**

1. The Parties agree that, where ESI items need to be redacted, they shall be produced solely in TIFF format with each redaction clearly indicated, except in the case of personal database files (e.g., MS Access), which shall be governed by ¶ II(C), *supra*. Any metadata fields reasonably available and unnecessary to protect the privilege protected by the redaction shall be provided. In some cases, MS Excel documents that need to be redacted may be redacted in native format if reasonably practicable; otherwise they will be produced in TIFF format.

2. If the items redacted and partially withheld from production are Excel-type spreadsheets as addressed in ¶ II(C), *supra*, and the native items are also withheld, to the extent reasonably practicable, each entire ESI item must be produced in TIFF format, including all unprivileged pages, hidden fields, and other information that does not print when opened as last saved by the custodian or end-user. For PowerPoint-type presentation decks, this shall include, but is not limited to, any speaker notes. For Excel-type spreadsheets, this shall include, but is not limited to, hidden rows and columns, all cell values, annotations, and notes. The producing Party shall

also make reasonable efforts to ensure that any spreadsheets produced only as TIFF images are formatted so as to be legible. For example, column widths should be formatted so that the numbers in the column will display rather than "##########."

3. If the items redacted and partially withheld from production are audio/visual files, the producing Party shall, to the extent reasonably practicable, provide the unredacted portions of the content. If the content is a voice recording, the Parties shall meet and confer to discuss the appropriate manner for the producing Party to produce the unredacted portion of the content.

D. **Email Collection and Processing:**

1. **Email Threading:** The Parties may use email thread suppression to avoid review and production of information contained within an existing email thread in another document being reviewed and produced, but under no circumstances will email thread suppression eliminate (a) the ability of a requesting Party to identify every custodian who had a copy of a produced document or email, or (b) remove from a production any unique branches and/or attachments contained within an email thread.

2. **Email Domains:** Excluded from any ESI search process shall be uniquely identifiable categories of documents, such as emails from domains typically associated with junk email, such as fantasy football-related emails, retailer advertising, and newsletters or alerts from non-industry sources. The Parties agree to disclose domain names excluded under this ¶ IV(D)(2) and to meet and confer on the timing for such disclosures.

E. **De-duplication:** A producing Party may de-duplicate any file globally (i.e., across Document Custodians, *see infra* ¶ V(B)(1)) or horizontally at the "family" level. If a requesting Party demonstrates a need for such information after receiving a production, the requesting Party shall identify by Bates number the document for which such information is needed, and the producing Party will make a reasonable effort to identify all custodians who were in possession of the de-duplicated document. Additionally, all BCC recipients whose names would have been included in the BCC metadata field, to the extent such metadata exists, but are excluded because of horizontal/global de-duplication, must be identified in the BCC metadata field specified in Appendix 1 to the extent such metadata exists. In the event of rolling productions of documents or ESI items, the producing Party will, as needed, supplement the load files with updated CustodianAll or CustodianOther information, as well as BCC information to the extent such metadata exists. Duplicate custodian information may be provided by a metadata "overlay" and will be provided by a producing Party after the Party has substantially completed its production of ESI.

1. Duplicate electronic documents shall be identified by a commercially accepted industry standard (e.g., MD5 or SHA-1 hash values) for binary file content. All electronic documents bearing an identical value are a duplicate group. The producing Party shall produce only one document image or native file for duplicate ESI documents within the duplicate group to the extent practicable. The producing Party is not obligated to extract or produce entirely duplicate ESI documents. Any other methodology for identification of duplicates, including email field selection for hash value creation, must be discussed with the requesting Party and approved in writing before implementation.

2. Duplicate messaging files shall be identified by a commercially accepted industry standard (e.g., MD5 hash values) for the email family, which includes the parent and email attachments. Duplicate messaging materials will be identified at a family level, including message and attachments(s). Email families bearing an identical value are considered a duplicate group. The producing Party shall produce only one document image or native file for duplicate emails within the duplicate group to the extent practicable.

F. **Zero-byte Files:** The Parties may filter out stand-alone files identified as zero-bytes in size that do not contain responsive file links or file names. If the requesting Party in good faith believes that a zero-byte file was withheld from production and contains information responsive to a request for production, the requesting Party may request that the producing Party produce the zero-byte file. The requesting Party may provide a Bates number to the producing Party of any document that suggests a zero-byte file was withheld from production and contains information responsive to a request for production.

G. **Microsoft "Auto" Feature:** To the extent reasonably practicable and technologically possible for a producing Party's vendor, Microsoft Excel (.xls) and Microsoft PowerPoint (.ppt) documents should be analyzed for the "auto" features, where documents have an automatically updated date and time in the document, file names, file paths, or similar information that when processed would be inaccurate for how the document was used in the ordinary course of business. If "auto date," "auto file name," "auto file path," or similar features are identified, the produced document shall be branded with the words "Auto Date," "Auto File Name," or "Auto File Path" formula used or similar words that describe the "auto" feature.

H. **Hidden Text:** ESI items processed after the execution date of this ESI Protocol Order shall be processed, to the extent practicable, in a manner that preserves hidden columns or rows, hidden text, worksheets, speaker notes, tracked changes, and comments.

I. **Embedded Objects:** Microsoft Excel (.xls) spreadsheets embedded in Microsoft Word documents will be extracted as separate documents and treated like attachments to the document. The Parties agree that other embedded objects, including, but not limited to, logos, icons, emoticons, and footers, may be culled from a document set and need not be produced as separate documents by a producing Party (e.g., such embedded objects will be produced within the document itself, rather than as separate attachments).

J. **Compressed Files:** Compression file types (i.e., .CAB, .GZ, .TAR, .Z, and .ZIP) shall be decompressed in a reiterative manner to ensure that a zip within a zip is decompressed into the lowest possible compression resulting in individual folders and/or files.

K. **Password-Protected, Encrypted, or Proprietary-Software Files:** With respect to any ESI items that are password-protected or encrypted, the producing Party will take reasonable steps based on industry standards to break the protection so that the documents can be reviewed and produced if appropriate. In the event that encrypted or password-protected documents, which are reasonably likely to be responsive to a document request, remain for a particular custodian after such reasonable efforts have been made, the producing Party shall advise the requesting Party. ESI that cannot be reviewed because proprietary software is necessary to view the ESI will be disclosed to a requesting Party, and the Parties shall meet and confer regarding the next steps, if any, with respect to such ESI.

V. PARAMETERS FOR CULLING AND REVIEWING ESI AND PAPER DOCUMENTS

A. **General Provisions:**

1. **Time Period:** Except as noted elsewhere in this ¶ V(A)(1), the Parties agree that they may limit the processing of discoverable information to that which was created, modified, sent, or received between January 1, 2007 and September 2, 2016 unless otherwise specified and agreed to by the Parties in writing. [redacted]

2. **Iterative Process:** The Parties and the Court plan to discuss search methodology and may amend this ESI Protocol Order or enter a separate Search Methodology Protocol in the future.

3. **Meet and Confer:** A requesting or producing Party may, in good faith, seek to expand or contract the scope of the search. Where such a request is made, the Parties will meet and confer and attempt in good faith to reach agreement as to the timing and conditions of such expansion or contraction. If the Parties cannot reach agreement, any dispute may be presented to the Court. All meet and confer sessions under this ¶ V(A)(3) will involve each Party's respective ESI Liaison and will give appropriate consideration to minimizing expense.

4. **Non-Waiver:** The Parties' discussion of proposed search terms does not preclude a Party from requesting additional search terms pursuant to the terms of this ESI Protocol Order as discovery and the Litigation progress nor does it preclude a Party from objecting to any such additional search terms requested.

B. **Document Custodians:**

1. **Document Custodians:** Each Party will disclose an initial list of proposed document custodians reflecting those employees with information and/or documents responsive to the agreed-on scope of Rule 34 requests ("Document Custodian(s)").

2. **Additional Document Custodians:** If, after the Parties identify initial Document Custodians, a requesting Party determines that an additional Document Custodian should be added, then the requesting Party shall advise the producing Party in writing of the proposed additional Document Custodian and the basis for the request. If the Parties have not agreed whether to add the Document Custodian within 30 days of the requesting Party's request for an additional Document Custodian, the Parties shall bring the matter to the Court via a joint letter brief.

3. Except by agreement of the Parties or by order of the Court, a producing Party is not required to add custodians after completion of the above phases.

C. **Use of Search Terms to Cull Unstructured ESI:**

1. The Parties may use search terms and other limiters, including, by way of example only, date ranges and email domains in metadata fields, as a means of limiting the volumes of information to be reviewed for responsiveness. To the extent that search terms are used to identify responsive ESI, a producing Party will notify the requesting Party of its intent to use search terms and disclose to the requesting Party (1) an initial list of search terms the producing Party intends to use and (2) whether the

producing Party intends to use different search terms with different custodians or data sets. Additionally, the Parties may elect to use a common set of search terms—one common set that applies to all Plaintiffs and one common set that applies to all Defendants. The Parties will cooperate in good faith regarding the disclosure and formulation of appropriate search terms and protocols to cull unstructured ESI.

2. **Addition or Removal of Search Terms After Initial Search Term Negotiation:** If, after the completion of the initial search methodology disclosures, a requesting or producing Party determines that any search terms should be added to or removed from the initial search term list, then the requesting or producing Party shall advise the affected Parties in writing of the proposed change(s) to the search term(s) and of the reason(s) for the proposed change(s).

3. Except by agreement of the Parties or by order of the Court, a producing Party is not required to add custodians or search terms after completion of the above phases.

D. **Use of Technology Assisted Review or Other Advanced Technology-Based Analytics to Cull Unstructured ESI:**

1. **Use of TAR:** A Party may use Technology Assisted Review ("TAR") to sort documents for linear review without disclosure of that use. If a Party elects to use TAR to cull or otherwise limit the volume of unstructured ESI subject to linear review, the parameters set forth in ¶ V(D)(2) shall apply.

2. **Parameters for use of TAR:**

   a. **Paper Documents:** The Parties agree to meet and confer to determine whether paper documents may be included in a TAR process.

   b. **The TAR Tool:** A producing Party shall describe to a requesting Party the vendor and the TAR technology or tool being used, including a description of the TAR tool s procedures.

   c. [The Parties and the Court continue to discuss the parameters for the use of TAR.]

3. A producing Party need not conduct any additional review of information subjected to, but not retrieved by, a TAR tool as part of the identification of the subset of information that will be subject to review and production.

E. **Electronic Non-Custodial Documents:**

1. **Producing Party's Non-Custodial Document Disclosures:** The producing Party will disclose a list of electronic "Non-Custodial" document sources (i.e., sources other than a Document Custodian's files) reasonably likely to contain responsive information sufficient to permit the requesting Party to determine (a) generally where and by whom the documents were maintained and (b) a general description of the types of documents in the particular Non-Custodial document storage location to the extent these categories of information are reasonably available.

2. **Non-Custodial Document Search Process:** As a general matter, the means of and parameters for culling ESI set forth in this Paragraph V apply to Non-Custodial ESI as well as to Custodial ESI. However, a producing Party may propose utilizing other culling technologies for Non-Custodial ESI by disclosing those no later than 14 days after a final decision to use these other culling technologies is made. A requesting Party may raise issues or objections to the other culling technology within 14 days of the disclosure. The Parties agree to meet and confer on any issues a requesting Party raises within this time period. A producing Party may not moot the question of whether or not proposed culling technology should be used by proceeding with use of the technique and incurring substantial costs in doing so, or if it does, it may not argue that such costs justify adopting its approach as opposed to the actual merits of the proposed culling technique. However, nothing in this ¶ V(E)(2) shall be construed to preclude substantial cost savings as relevant to the "merits" and justification of the proposed approach.

F. **Structured Data:** To the extent a response to discovery requires production of discoverable ESI contained in a structured database, the Parties shall meet and confer in an attempt to agree upon a set of queries to be made for discoverable information and generate a report in a reasonably usable and exportable electronic file (e.g., Excel or CSV format) for review by the requesting Party. Upon review of the report, the requesting Party may make reasonable requests for additional information to explain the database schema, codes, abbreviations, and different report formats or to request specific data from identified fields.

G. **Custodial Cellphone & Personal Communications Data:**

1. **Cellphones:** For Document Custodians agreed on by the Parties or ordered by the Court, a producing Party will take reasonable steps to identify whether any unique responsive communications are located on any cellphones in the possession, custody, or control of the producing Party. Unless agreed otherwise, the following shall govern the review and production of unique, responsive, and non-privileged communications for cellphone-based data for the agreed or ordered Document Custodians with

respect to cellphones in the possession, custody, or control of the producing Party.

a. Prior to any culling of the cellphone data, a producing Party will disclose the following to the extent reasonably possible: (1) to the extent not already provided, a list of cellphone number(s) used by the Document Custodian for work purposes, if any, (2) the name of the phone carrier that provided service for each identified phone number, (3) the type of phone, including brand and model number, if known, (4) a list of installed communications-related applications on the Document Custodian's cellphone, including ephemeral messaging applications (e.g., SnapChat, Confide, and Signal), Facebook Messenger, and other such applications if such applications are used for work purposes; and (5) whether or not the producing Party claims that a cellphone used by the Document Custodian for work purposes is not within its possession, custody, or control.

b. A producing Party will review the following sources of information on a cellphone, to the extent reasonably available, to identify unique, responsive, and discoverable information:

i. **Cellphone Call and Voicemail Logs:** The logs of any calls made/received and voicemails left on a cellphone that the Document Custodian used for work purposes, if any, if the cellphone is in the possession, custody, or control of a producing Party.

ii. **Text Messages:** All text messages and/or iMessages on the cellphone device used for work purposes or contained in available backups/archives associated with the device, if any, if the cellphone is in the possession, custody, or control of a producing Party.

c. **"Contacts":** A Document Custodian's relevant contacts (e.g., MS Outlook Contacts or cellphone-based contacts) will be exported to MS Excel (or .csv) with all reasonably available metadata fields. For mobile devices that are owned by the Document Custodian and used for personal purposes, if the device is in the possession, custody, or control of a producing Party, a producing Party is entitled to redact or withhold information from the contacts file that does not relate to the Document Custodian's work—including, but not limited to, the name and contact information for any family or friends not involved [redacted] If, after reviewing the redactions, the requesting Party believes that more information is needed about the redactions, then the Parties will meet and confer regarding the information redacted, and the producing Party shall provide explanations for information redacted or withheld. Any document produced with redactions pursuant to this ¶ V(G)(1)(c) shall maintain the electronic search capabilities of the other data in the spreadsheet.

2. **Social Media Data:** If a Document Custodian confirms that he or she (1) used Social Media for business purposes and (2) used that Social Media to communicate with an employee of another Defendant or otherwise regarding a subject relevant to the Litigation and included within a Request for Production, subject to objections to that Request, then the requested communication(s) must be produced if it is reasonably accessible, in the producing Party's possession, custody, or control, and not withheld as privileged and/or as illegal to produce under applicable privacy laws. The Parties shall meet and confer to the extent there are any issues with respect to the format of such Social Media data.

VI. CLAIMS OF PRIVILEGE AND REDACTIONS

A. **Production of Privilege Logs:** Except as provided otherwise below, for any document withheld in its entirety or produced but redacted, the producing Party will produce privilege/redaction logs in MS Excel format or any other format that permits electronic sorting and searching. The Parties plan to meet and confer regarding rolling production deadlines, including prioritizing the production of certain Document Custodians' documents. For such prioritized Document Custodians, a producing Party will produce a privilege/redaction log for any documents withheld or redacted within 53 days of substantially completing production of those Document Custodians' documents. A producing Party will produce a privilege/redaction log for any withheld or redacted documents not previously logged within 53 days of Substantial Completion of Document Productions (*see* Dkt. 388 at 2).

B. **Exclusions from Logging Potentially Privileged Documents:** The following categories of documents do not need to be contained on a producing Party's initial privilege log, unless good cause exists to require that a Party do so.

1. Information generated before January 1, 2007 and after September 2, 2016, except as provided in ¶ V(A)(1). This provision does not apply to third Parties to the Litigation.
2. Any communications exclusively between a producing Party and its outside counsel, an agent of outside counsel other than the Party, any non-testifying experts in connection with specific litigation, or with respect to information protected by Fed. R. Civ. P. 26(b)(4), testifying experts in connection with specific litigation.
3. Any privileged materials or work product created by or specifically at the direction of a Party's outside counsel, an agent of outside counsel other than the Party, any non-testifying experts in connection with specific

litigation, or with respect to information protected by Fed. R. Civ. P. 26(b)(4), testifying experts in connection with specific litigation.

C. **Privilege Log Requirements:**

1. **Metadata Log:** To the extent applicable, each Party's privilege log only needs to provide objective metadata (to the extent it is reasonably available and does not reflect privileged or protected information) and an indication of the privilege or protection being asserted.

a. Objective metadata includes the following (as applicable to the document types as shown in Appendix A):

i. A unique privilege log identifier
ii. Custodian
iii. CustodianOther or CustodianAll (if applicable)
iv. File Name
v. Email Subject
vi. Author
vii. From
viii. To
ix. CC
x. BCC
xi. Date Sent
xii. Date Received
xiii. Date Created

b. In addition to the objective metadata fields, a Party must also include a field on its privilege log entitled "Attorney/Description of Privileged Material" if the basis for the privilege asserted is not apparent from the objective metadata (e.g., the name of the attorney will be provided if not included in the objective metadata). Further, a Party must manually populate on its privilege log an author and date for any withheld document where that information is not provided by the objective metadata, unless such information is not reasonably discernable from the document or the information is not necessary to evaluate the claim of privilege in light of the metadata that is discernable and/or the information provided in the Attorney/Description of Privileged Material field.

c. With respect to the "Email Subject" or "File Name" field, the producing Party may substitute a description of the document where the contents of these fields may reveal privileged information. In the privilege log(s), the producing Party shall identify each instance in which it has modified the content of the "Email Subject" or "File Name" field.

d. Should a receiving Party, in good faith, have reason to believe a particular entry on a metadata-generated privilege log is responsive and does not reflect privileged discoverable information, the receiving Party may request, and the producing Party will not unreasonably refuse to create, a privilege log for that entry in compliance with Fed. R. Civ. P. 26(b)(5).

2. **Email Chains:** If there is more than one branch of (i.e., more than one unique group of recipients of) an email thread, each branch will be individually logged; however, each individual email within the thread need not be logged if the recipients of the email chain are all identical. A Party asserting privilege over a chain of emails may produce only a single redacted copy of such email chain consistent with ¶ VI(D) to the extent some portions are only partially privileged, except that any unique branches of the email chain must also either be produced in redacted form or included on the metadata privilege log.

D. **Documents Redacted for Privilege:** As an initial production matter, redacted documents need not be logged as long as (a) for emails, the objective metadata (i.e., to, from, cc, bcc, recipients, date, and time, unless the privilege or protection is contained in these fields) is not redacted, and the reason for the redaction, including the nature of the privilege asserted, is noted on the face of the document (for redacted documents where the subject matter is not decipherable as a result of redactions, a description of the contents of the document that is sufficient to understand the subject matter of the document may be requested); and (b) for non-email documents, the reason for the redaction is noted on the face of the document in the redacted area. In accordance with this ¶ VI(D), the producing Party will undertake reasonable efforts to make limited, line-by-line redactions of privileged or work product information. After receipt of the production, the requesting Party may request in good faith that the producing Party create a privilege log for specific redacted documents. Electronic documents that are redacted shall be identified as such in a "redaction" field in the accompanying data load file.

E. **Challenges to Privilege Claims:** Following the receipt of a privilege/redaction log, a requesting Party may identify, in writing (by Bates/unique identified number), the particular documents that it believes require further explanation. The producing Party shall endeavor to respond to such a request within 14 days. If a Party challenges a request for further information, the Parties shall meet and confer to try to reach a mutually agreeable solution. If they cannot agree, the matter may be brought to the Court.

F. **"Relevancy" Redactions:** A Party may redact irrelevant information that is highly sensitive, medical, or personal information (e.g., health information or Social Security Numbers).

VII. <u>CLAWBACK ORDER</u>

A. **Non-Waiver:** Pursuant to Federal Rule of Evidence 502(d), the production of any material or information shall not be deemed to waive any privilege or work product protection in the Litigation or in any other federal or state proceeding. Nothing in this Paragraph VII is intended to or shall serve to limit a Party's right to conduct a review of any material or information for relevance, responsiveness, and/or segregation of privileged and/or protected information before production, subject to ¶ VII(B)(1) below. The Parties stipulate that the Court should enter a Rule 502(d) Order to this end, which shall be interpreted to provide the maximum protection allowed by Rule 502(d).

B. **Assertion of a Clawback:** Any Party or non-Party may request the return of any produced material or information on the grounds of privilege or work product protection by identifying it, stating the basis for withholding such material or information from production, and providing any other information that would be listed on a supplemental privilege log, subject to ¶ VII(B)(1) below.

1. **Clawbacks Before Depositions:** If a Party attempts to clawback a document authored or received by an individual who is scheduled for a deposition within 30 days of the date of the deposition, and the propriety of the clawback is not resolved pursuant to ¶ VII(C)(2) prior to the date of the deposition, then the Parties will meet and confer on the appropriate course of action, which may, but need not necessarily, include:

a. rescheduling the deposition until the issue is resolved by the Court;

b. conferring prior to the deposition to determine if the document may be used in the deposition subject to agreed-upon limitations;

c. calling the Court if the clawback is made during the deposition to determine if immediate resolution is possible; and/or

d. allowing the Party resisting the clawback to recall the deponent for the sole and exclusive purpose of questioning the deponent on the document at issue if the Court subsequently determines the clawback was improper (if exercised, recalling the deponent for this purpose will not count against the total number of depositions or deposition hours to which the Party resisting the clawback is entitled).

C. **Clawback Process:** Federal Rule of Civil Procedure 26(B)(5)(b) shall govern the clawback of produced documents or information on the grounds of privilege or work product protection. If a Party or non-Party requests the return of such produced material or information then in the custody of one or more Parties, the possessing Parties shall within seven (7) business days:

1. Destroy or return to the requesting Party or non-Party the produced material or information and all copies thereof, and expunge from any other document or material, information derived solely from the produced material or information; or

2. Notify the producing Party or non-Party that it wishes to challenge the claim of privilege or work product protection and has sequestered the material until the issue can be resolved. The Parties agree to meet and

confer regarding the claim of privilege. If, at the conclusion of the meet and confer process, the Parties are still not in agreement, they may bring the issue to the Court. A Party challenging a clawback request under this ¶ VII(C)(2) may use the content of the clawed-back document for the purpose of filing a motion with the Court under seal that challenges whether or not the document is privileged or work product only.

VIII. MISCELLANEOUS PROVISIONS

A. **Inaccessible ESI:** If a producing Party asserts that certain categories of ESI that are reasonably likely to contain responsive information are inaccessible or otherwise unnecessary under the circumstances, or if the requesting Party asserts that, following production, certain ESI is not reasonably usable, the Parties shall meet and confer with their respective technology experts to discuss resolving such assertions. If the Parties cannot resolve any such disputes after such a meet and confer has taken place, the issue shall be presented to the Court for resolution.

B. **Assertion of Undue Burden or Cost:** If a Party objects to producing requested information on the grounds that such information is not reasonably accessible because of undue burden or cost, or because production in the requested format will create undue burden or cost, the producing Party will inform the requesting Party of the reason(s) why the requested form of production would impose an undue burden or is unreasonably costly. The requesting Party will have 14 days from receipt of such notice to propose an alternative means of compliance with the request and failure to do so will result in waiver. Prior to a Party producing ESI in a format not requested and/or agreed to by the requesting Party, (1) the Parties will meet and confer regarding the issue, and, failing resolution, the Parties will (2) file a joint letter brief with the Court regarding the issue. Nothing in this ¶ VIII(B) limits the rights of a producing Party to object to any discovery request for any reason.

C. **Objections Preserved:** Nothing in this ESI Protocol Order shall be interpreted to require disclosure of information protected by the attorney-client privilege, work product doctrine, or any other applicable privilege or immunity. Except as provided expressly herein, the Parties do not waive any objections as to the production, discoverability, authenticity, admissibility, or confidentiality of documents and ESI.

D. **Variations or Modifications:** Variations from this ESI Protocol Order may be required. Any practice or procedure set forth herein may be varied by agreement of all affected Plaintiffs and all affected Defendants, which will be confirmed in writing. In the event a producing Party determines that a variation or modification is appropriate or necessary to facilitate the timely and economical production of documents or ESI, the producing Party will notify the requesting Party of the variation or modification. Upon request by the requesting Party, those Parties will meet and confer to address any issues in a reasonable and timely manner prior to seeking Court intervention.

Appendix 1: ESI Metadata and Coding Fields

Field Name[1]	Populated For (Email, Edoc, Calendar, Contact, Cellphone, or All)	Field Description
BegBates	All	Control Numbers.
EndBates	All	Control Numbers.
BegAttach	All	Control Numbers (First production Bates number of the first document of the family).
EndAttach	All	Control Numbers (Last production Bates number of the last document of the family).
Custodian	All	Custodian name (ex. John Doe).
CustodianOther or CustodianAll	All	All custodians who were in possession of a de-duplicated document besides the individual identified in the "Custodian" field.
LogicalPath	All ESI Items	The director structure of the original file(s). Any container name is included in the path.
Hash Value	All	The MD5 or SHA-1 hash value.
NativeFile	All	Native File Link.
Email Thread ID	Email	Unique identification number that permits threading of email conversations. For instance, unique MS Outlook identification number ("PR_CONVERSATION_INDEX") is 22 bytes in length, followed by zero or more child blocks each 5 bytes in length, that facilitates use of email threading.
Thread Index	Email	Message header identifier, distinct from "PR_Conversation_Index", that permits threading of email chains in review software.
EmailSubject	Email	Subject line of email.
DateSent	Email	Date email was sent.
DateMod	Email, Edoc	Date the document was modified.
TimeSent	Email	Time email was sent.
TimeZoneUsed	All	Time zone used to process data during document collection and processing.
ReceiveTime	Email	Time email was received.
To	Email	All recipients that were included on the "To" line of the email.
From	Email	The name and email address of the sender of the email.
CC	Email	All recipients that were included on the "CC" line of the email.
BCC	Email	All recipients that were included on the "BCC" line of the email.
DateCreated	Edoc	Date the document was created.
FileName	Email, Edoc	File name of the edoc or email.

[1] Field Names can vary from system to system and even between different versions of systems. Thus, Parties are to be guided by these Field Names and Descriptions when identifying the metadata fields to be produced for a given document pursuant to this ESI Protocol Order.

Field Name[1]	Populated For (Email, Edoc, Calendar, Contact, Cellphone, or All)	Field Description
Title	Edoc	Any value populated in the Title field of the document properties.
Subject	Edoc	Any value populated in the Subject field of the document properties.
Author	Edoc	Any value populated in the Author field of the document properties.
DocExt	All	File extension of the document.
TextPath	All	Relative path to the document level text file.
Redacted	All	"X," "Y," "Yes," and "True" are all acceptable indicators that the document is redacted. Otherwise, blank.
Paper	All	"Y" if document is scanned from hard copy in connection with the collection and production of documents in this matter.
Confidentiality	All	Indicates if document has been designated as "Confidential" or "Highly Confidential" under the Protective Order.

Appendix F

Comprehensive Custodial Interview

Name of Custodian: ______________________________
Date: ______________________________

❑ The facts of the matter for which the Litigation Hold has been instituted have been explained thoroughly to Custodian.
❑ Custodian understands the duty to preserve relevant electronic information whether stored on or off the network and the consequences for failing to do so.
❑ Custodian agrees to take all reasonable steps to identify and locate information in electronic or hard copy format relevant to the matter at hand in order that the information may be preserved and secured.
❑ Custodian agrees to suspend normal delete and destruction of electronic mail messages or other electronic information until notified that the information has been preserved and secured.
❑ Custodian agrees to continue to preserve relevant information until notified that the information currently on the system has been preserved and will continue to preserve future generated information until the Litigation Hold is terminated.

Preservation & Litigation Hold

1. Did you receive the Litigation Hold Notice?
2. When did you receive Litigation Hold Notice?
3. Do you understand the notice?
4. Do you understand what data might potentially be relevant to the suit which is the subject of the hold?
5. What steps did you take to identify and locate the data which might be potentially relevant?
6. Have you altered, modified, deleted, or otherwise utilized the data since being notified of the hold?
7. If so, what have you done?
8. Do you know whether the data identified by you as potentially relevant data has been preserved by IT?

INQUIRY FOR LOCATING SOURCES OF POTENTIALLY RELEVANT INFORMATION

1. Please circle the items below and provide additional information to the right if they are sources of potentially relevant electronic documents, files or emails:

Area	**Location, Files, Folders, Titles, etc.**
Network	
Document Management System	
Shared Drives	
Databases	
Intranet/Extranet (Sharepoint)	
Other (Wikis)	
Local PC	
Desktop or Laptop (Office)	
My Documents	
E-mails:	
Server based	
Archived to local PC	
C:/drive	
Other	
Personal PC or Laptop	
My Documents	
E-mails	
C:/drive	
Other	
PDA (type)	
Cell phone	
Voicemail/VOIP	
Portable Media	
Flash drives	
CDs	
DVDs	
Floppy disks/diskettes	
Audiotapes/audio files	
Videotapes	
Hard drives	

Area	**Location, Files, Folders, Titles, etc.**
Legacy hardware (old PCs)	
Legacy PDA or cell	
Backups	
Web Based Sources	
List Servs	
Personal e-mail accounts	
Instant messages	
Pin-to-pin	
Social Media (blogs, Chat Rooms, Face Book, Twitter)	
Other	

2. Please identify other potentially relevant computer files on the network where they are located and how they are titled and organized.
3. Please identify where potentially relevant electronic data off network is located and how it is organized.
4. Please identify the software applications (MS Word, Outlook) used by you to create and/or store potentially relevant information.
5. Please identify any technical issues that may have impacted potentially relevant electronic information (computer crash, loss of power, migration to new software platform, replacement of hard ware, purge recycle bin, etc.)

❑ Custodian has identified the following **categories of documents** (electronic and hard copy) as potentially relevant to the pending matter:

____

____

____

____

____

____

____

____

____

❑ Custodian took the **following steps** in an effort to locate potentially relevant documents:

❑ Custodian understands that **sanctions for spoliation** may be imposed for altering, modifying, deleting or destroying potentially relevant information.

❑ Custodian (is/is not) aware of any **potentially relevant documents that have been altered, modified, deleted or destroyed** since being notified of the Litigation Hold. If Custodian is aware of such documents, please list them below and explain how or why that occurred:

❑ Custodian (has/has not) recently received **a new office computer, PDA, cell phone or other device** where potentially relevant information may have been stored. If so, please identify the device and explain why the device was replaced and what happened to the **prior device** if known.

❑ Custodian (is/is not) aware of any **legacy systems** (old computers, PDAs or other device) where potentially relevant information may be stored. If so, please identify the legacy device and its current location.

❑ Custodian (is/is not) aware of any **backup tape** or other backup storage device where potentially relevant information may be stored. If so, please identify the backup device and its current location.

❑ Custodian's **office computer** is used to access potentially relevant information in the following locations:

Y/N Document Management System. If so, provide information sufficient to retrieve potentially relevant information.

Y/N Other Databases. If so, provide information sufficient to isolate potentially relevant information.

Y/N Office E-mail Box (Inbox, Sent Items, Delete Items, Recycle Bin, Calendar, Contacts, Task List, Personal Folders). If Personal Folders contain potentially relevant information, please provide the names of the folders.

If Custodian's e-mail box needs to be searched electronically for potentially relevant information, the following limiting parameters (key words, dates, author/recipient) should be applied:

(1) Names of **other custodians** who were involved in relevant e-mail communications.

____

____

____

____

____

____

____

____

(2) Relevant **time period** for relevant e-mail communications.

____

____

(3) **Key words** to be used to locate relevant e-mail communications.

____

____

____

____

____

____

____

____

Y/N <u>Shared Network Drives</u>. If so, provide file path and folder/file names where potentially relevant information is stored and other persons who have access to the shared drives.

____

____

____

Y/N My Computer. If so, provide file path (e.g., I: drive), folder names and/or document names and application (MS Word, Adobe, Excel, etc.) for potentially relevant information.

Y/N Archives. Provide details.

Y/N Internet History. **If Internet cookies, temp/cached files, or history contains potentially relevant information, notify IT immediately so that the information can be preserved.**

Y/N Other. Provide names of other sources accessed by Custodian's office computer where potentially relevant documents may be stored (e.g., intranet, extranet, PC desktop, etc.).

____

____

____

____

____

____

____

____

____

____

❑ Custodian (has/does not have) a **PDA** where potentially relevant information may be stored.

Y/N iPhone/Blackberry (Inbox, Sent Items, Deleted Items, Calendar, Contacts, Text Messages, Voice Mail). **If potentially relevant information exists on Custodian's iPhone /Blackberry, contact IT immediately so the information can be preserved.**

❑ Custodian (has/does not have) a **cell phone** where potentially relevant information may be stored. **If potentially relevant information exists on Custodian's cell phone, contact IT immediately so the information can be preserved.**

❑ Custodian (has/does not have) **office Voice Mail** that contains potentially relevant messages. **If potentially relevant information exists on Custodian's office Voice Mail, contact IT immediately so the information can be preserved.**

❑ Custodian (has/does not have) a **personal computer** where potentially relevant information may be stored. If so, provide details.

❑ Custodian (has/does not have) a **personal e-mail account** where potentially relevant information may be stored. If so, provide details.

❑ Custodian (has/does not have) a **personal cell phone, voice mail system or answering machine** where potentially relevant messages are stored. If so, provide details.

____

____

____

____

____

❑ Custodian (has/does not have) **portable storage media** where potentially relevant information may be stored. If so, please complete the following chart:

Portable Storage Media	Content	Current Location
Flash drive(s)		
CD(s)		
DVD(s)		
Floppy disk/diskette(s)		
Audiotape (dictaphone)		
Videotape(s)		
Hard drives		
Other (camera, iPod, etc.)		

❑ Custodian (is/is not) aware of **outside sources** where potentially relevant information may be stored. If so, please complete the following chart:

Outside Source	Content	Web address/user name and password
List Serv(s)		
Chat Room(s)		
Blog(s)		
Other (Facebook, Twitter, Wikis, etc.)		

❑ Custodian (is/is not) aware of any **other sources** of potentially relevant electronic information. If so, provide details.

____

____

____

____

____
____
____
____
____
____

❑ Custodian has taken steps to identify, locate and secure potentially relevant information in **hard copy format**, and has instructed all persons with access to these documents that they are subject to the preservation duty outlined in the Litigation Hold for the pending matter.

❑ Custodian has been notified of all personnel subject to the Litigation Hold instituted for the pending matter. **Other possible custodians** of potentially relevant information known to Custodian include the following:

____
____
____
____
____
____
____
____
____
____

____
Custodian Signature and Date

____
Interviewer Signature and Date

Appendix G

Sample Legal Hold Notice #1

NOTICE

<u>Privileged and Confidential</u>

<u>Attorney-Client Communication</u>

This Notice is being sent on behalf of [Responsible Attorney and title]

Please Acknowledge Receipt of This Notice and Compliance by Clicking One of the Buttons below the Notice.

[Insert organization name] is currently involved in litigation with [insert party name(s) here]. In addition, [insert organization name] believes or has reason to believe that it may become involved in litigation with [insert potential parties or other third parties or individuals here].

During the course of this litigation, we will be asked to produce documents relating to the claims made by us and by the opposing party. It is critical that documents relevant to these requests be kept. Failure to preserve documents that we are required to produce could provide significant obstacles to a thorough investigation and defense of litigation and could result in serious fines or other penalties. The documents we must preserve include paper documents as well as electronic documents (including all email messages and attachments, word processing documents, spreadsheets, calendar entries, databases, computer drawings, instant messages, text messages or any other documents or files created on [insert organization name]'s or your home computer systems). ***You should not make any decisions regarding the importance of any documents, but rather <u>preserve all information</u> that mentions or relates to the facts of this matter.***

The time period primarily at issue in this case is [insert time period covered by hold]. While this relevant date range may change as the case proceeds, this is a good starting point for accessing the volume of documents to be preserved.

Effective immediately, it is critical that you do not delete, over-write, or otherwise alter or destroy any documents or files (print or electronic) which may be relevant to this case. This includes any email related to [insert name of opposing parties here], including any documentation related to [insert specific facts of situation here].

[Insert Counsel or specific person] will be in touch with each of you to identify the sources of any information you have either in paper or electronically so that we can ensure all relevant and responsive information is preserved. In the meantime, if you know of issues that we need to consider related to keeping both paper and electronic information for this case, or other individuals or third parties that should be listed on this notice but are not, please contact me at [insert email address for contact person/counsel].

In addition, in the event that you are contacted by anyone outside of [insert organization name] to discuss this matter, you are to direct all calls to me at [insert phone number of contact].

Thank you for your cooperation. Please do not hesitate to call me with questions. As the production of email regarding this dispute will likely be necessary, we ask that you not email either internally or externally regarding the subject of the dispute, even to discuss this hold. All discussions should be conducted via telephone or in person.

INSERT OUTLOOK BUTTONS FOR:

I have read the notice and will comply

I do not have any responsive information

I have questions, please contact me

Appendix H

Sample Legal Hold Notice #2

ATTORNEY-CLIENT COMMUNICATION
PRIVILEGED AND CONFIDENTIAL
ATTORNEY WORK PRODUCT

MEMORANDUM

TO:

FROM:

DATE:

RE: Preservation of documents and electronic data relating to ________________

This memorandum (sometimes known as a "litigation hold") will confirm the obligations of __________________________ in regard to the preservation of evidence relevant to the lawsuit commenced recently by _____________ in United States Federal Court, District of ______________.

This memorandum is to confirm our request that all paper documents and electronic data contained in the Company's computer systems (and any related personal systems) be immediately preserved, as those documents and data may be a potentially important source of discovery and evidence in the litigation of this case. As such, the Company is required by law to take steps to ensure that all paper documents (including but not limited to drafts of documents) ***and*** all electronic data that are potentially relevant to this matter are preserved. To satisfy our legal obligations, we require your assistance in preserving electronic and hard-copy data as described herein.

LITIGATION HOLD:

The Company and all of its employees must preserve and retain (i.e., do not alter, delete or otherwise modify) any electronic data and/or paper documents that are or may be relevant to the matter. Relevant data includes, but is not necessarily limited to:

The preceding list is illustrative of the types of documents that must be preserved, and the instruction to preserve this information must be given to any and all employees, officers, directors, agents, contractors, or any other representatives of the Company who may possess or have access to these documents or information. Any question you may have as to the relevance of a particular document, file, email, electronic data compilation, or other materials should be resolved in favor of preservation and retention. Failure to preserve relevant information could result in significant penalties against the Company.

In identifying and preserving potentially responsive paper documents, please keep in mind that this directive is not limited to the "final version" of paper documents. Rather, this directive covers drafts of potentially responsive documents and includes all types of documents (letters, typed or hand written notes, memoranda, reports, studies, printed spreadsheets, Post-its, etc.). This directive also covers paper documents that are kept in departmental or central files or in off-site storage. In addition, be advised that the Company must retain a paper document even if someone other than the Company has or is supposed to have retained a copy of the same paper document. For example, if you receive a meeting agenda that contains information that is potentially relevant to the matter, you must retain your copy of the agenda even if the individual who supervises the meeting states that he or she is keeping an official copy of the agenda. Finally, be advised that if you have a paper copy of an electronic record, you must retain ***both*** the paper document and the electronic record. Regularly scheduled disposition of potentially responsive discovery materials ***must be suspended immediately and remain suspended*** until you receive further notice.

In identifying and preserving electronic data, please keep in mind that "electronic data" includes, but is not limited to, all text files (including word processing documents and presentations) saved anywhere on the Company network, any hard drive, any shared drive, any C: drive, any "My Documents" directory, Company's intranet and extranets, spreadsheets, email, instant messaging, blogs, databases, calendars, computer system activity logs, internet usage files, and network access information.

Further, the Company's computer network includes, but is not limited to, all workstations, laptops, network servers, blackberries, other hand-held devices, voicemail, and backup tapes. Again, any questions as to the scope of preservation must be resolved in favor of preservation and retention.

At individual work stations, this directive requires the Company to preserve and retain all potentially relevant electronic information stored on hard drives and all potentially relevant email contained in each employee's electronic mail (e-mail) mailbox and archive folders, as well as any public email folders. No one at the Company should be allowed to copy, forward, delete, trash, recycle (or empty the recycle bin), or otherwise affect the potentially relevant email. Any such action could affect the metadata associated with the electronic data.

At the network and systems administration level, we ask that any "janitorial" functions be disabled immediately. Additionally, the Company's record retention policy should be suspended with regard to potentially relevant documents. No relevant or potentially relevant documents should be disposed of regardless of any retention period defined in that policy. Any similar policy or practices regarding the destruction or retention of documents, formal or informal, must likewise suspended.

We appreciate your cooperation and understanding. These steps are necessary to ensure that the Company is in full compliance with the rules governing the litigation process. We will make every effort to minimize the disruption of your routine and business.

If you need any assistance in preserving electronically-stored information, please contact either of us at your earliest convenience.

This memorandum is a confidential attorney-client communication. Unless otherwise instructed, you should not distribute or disclose the contents of this memorandum to anyone, nor should you discuss the memorandum with anyone other than attorneys. All written communications relating to the contents of this memorandum should be clearly marked "ATTORNEY-CLIENT COMMUNICATION – PRIVILEGED AND CONFIDENTIAL."

Appendix I

Sample Legal Hold Notice #3

DOCUMENT PRESERVATION NOTICE

PLEASE READ IMMEDIATELY

TO: [***Employees who may be in possession, custody, or control of relevant documents***]

FROM:

CC: [***In-House Legal, IT, Human Resources, and Records Management Personnel***]

DATE:

RE: Document Preservation Notice

As you may be aware, (the "Matter"). [DESCRIBE MATTER]

In connection with the Matter, the Company is legally obligated to take steps to preserve all potentially relevant information, including hard-copy documents and all forms of electronically stored information ("ESI") that could relate in any way to the topics listed in Section II below ("Relevant Material"). You are receiving this Notice because you may possess, manage or control Relevant Material that must be preserved. Please contact me immediately if you believe you have received this Notice in error.

Please read the entire Notice and follow the instructions carefully. **Your compliance is mandatory**. When you have finished reading the Notice, please follow the steps contained in Section IV below to acknowledge that you have read, understand and will comply with these instructions. If you have any questions regarding the contents of this Notice and how best to comply with it, including questions concerning which documents need to be preserved, please contact me by email or call me on my cell phone at _____ or at the office at _______. If you have any questions related to how to preserve relevant email or any other electronic materials, including information located on personal devices or email accounts, please contact, Director of IT.

This is a **privileged and confidential** communication being circulated by the Company's legal department in consultation with our outside counsel. You should take precautions to keep this Notice confidential and should not share it with others.

The obligations described in this Notice supersede any routine retention or discard procedures that you currently follow and are ongoing until you are explicitly directed otherwise that this Notice is no longer in effect. If you receive another directive of any kind, including those related to company document retention practices or other litigation, you should not assume that the directive overrides or modifies the instructions here.

I. Your Obligations

Until further written notice, you must not destroy, discard, alter, modify, or delete any Relevant Material that was created, modified, sent, or received on or after __________, including drafts, work papers, personal notes, emails (both sent and received), and other electronically stored documents. This obligation applies both to existing documents and to documents that you may create or receive in the future. This obligation also applies to documents for which you believe duplicate copies may exist in other employees' files.

If you regularly delete emails or other documents that may constitute Relevant Material in the ordinary course of your work routine, you must immediately cease that practice. If you are concerned that certain Relevant Material may be deleted or destroyed in the ordinary course of business, please contact me immediately. For instance, if you are aware of automated procedures in place that may result in the deletion of Relevant Material without manual intervention, please let me know so that we can work with the IT department to ensure that such procedures are disabled. Failure to preserve Relevant Material in whatever format it exists could present significant obstacles to our positions in this Matters and could result in serious fines or other penalties. Please keep this Notice close at hand and refer to it often to ensure that you meet the preservation requirements.

For now, you are only obligated to keep these materials as-is. You should not begin to segregate or collect relevant documents at this time as doing so may alter the documents' metadata. If additional steps need to be taken to review, segregate or collect the documents and data that you retain, you will be contacted individually either by a member of the Company's legal department or by an attorney with _______, our outside counsel. Except for those discussions, you should avoid discussing this Matter with anyone, **including other employees**.

II. Subject Matter of Materials to Be Preserved

Any Relevant Material (in whatever form it exists, whether paper or electronic) must be preserved. The categories of information that are potentially relevant and thus must be preserved include, but *are not limited to,* all communications, documents, and/or information regarding the events, subject matter, and circumstances related to:

[MATTER SPECIFIC TOPICS]

Please note that this list of topics represents only our best assessment at this time of the topics and kinds of information that could potentially be relevant to this dispute. *You should interpret these categories broadly. If you have any doubt or questions regarding whether certain materials should be preserved, always err on the side of caution and preserve the information.*

III. Possible Forms and Locations of Relevant Information

Information in both paper and electronic format should be retained if it relates to the subject matter of the dispute described above, **including any relevant documents or information that you create or receive after the date of this Notice.** All information related to the topics above, including both working/draft copies and formal business records, must be retained. Likewise, you must retain any relevant documents that you may have inherited from another former or current employee or that you may have transferred to a personal device to facilitate working remotely.

The following materials must be saved if they contain potentially relevant information, regardless of where they may physically reside:

- emails and attachments; calendar entries, meeting invitations, and contacts; Microsoft Word, Excel, PowerPoint, Access, Project, and Visio documents; PDF files; photographs and images; e-faxes; text messages, instant messages, and voicemails; video, audio, and other multimedia files; databases, data extracts, and reports; and social media content.
- hard-copies of letters, reports, agreements, internal/external communications, correspondence, memoranda, calendars, journals, summaries or records of conversations or work assignments, formal/informal notes (typed or handwritten), envelopes, books, bulletins, and diaries, including copies of such documents that are not identical duplicates of the originals (e.g., with highlighting, handwritten comments, or margin notations).

Relevant documents may be found on a diverse array of data sources, including but not limited to:

- Corporate desktop or laptop computers; personal or departmental file shares; server-side email mailboxes (including one's "Inbox," "Deleted Items," "Sent Items," or any other subfolder); email archive files (e.g., PST or NSF files); optical disks (including CDs and DVDs), removable thumb drives or external hard drives, and other types of portable electronic storage media; backup tapes and other disaster-recovery systems; and internet, blog, intranet, extranet, portal, social media, or cloud-based sites and services; and Blackberries or other company-issued mobile devices
- Personal computers; personal iPhones, Android devices, or other smartphones; personal iPads or other tablet devices; personal email accounts (e.g., Gmail, Yahoo, Hotmail); thumb drives; social media sites (e.g., Facebook); and cloud-based storage locations (e.g., Dropbox).

This list is not all-inclusive and is intended to provide you with general guidelines regarding the possible forms and locations of potentially relevant materials. You should preserve any Relevant Material regardless of its form or location. If there are other employees who maintain certain files for you that may be relevant to this litigation, please notify me immediately.

IV. Certification of Compliance

Compliance with the procedures outlined in this Notice is critical, and any failure to comply could result in serious ramifications for the Company and for you. Within three (3) days of receiving this Notice, please send me an email stating that you acknowledge receiving this Notice and that you understand your obligations. Please include a list of any other employees you believe may have potentially relevant information in their possession, but do not forward this Notice to them on your own.

Thank you for your prompt attention to, and ongoing cooperation with, this matter.

Appendix J

Sample Review Protocol

ATTORNEY WORK PRODUCT
DO NOT DISTRIBUTE
PRIVILEGED & CONFIDENTIAL

MEMORANDUM

TO: Document Defendants' Discovery Team

FROM: Attorney

DATE: January 23, 2023

RE: Review for Plaintiff v. Defendants

This memorandum is intended to provide an overview of the relevant issues, people, and documents related to the above-captioned matter (the "Action") to assist you with reviewing and coding documents produced by Defendants. For your general review, we will also include copies of: (1) the Complaint in this matter (with Ex. A, which contains an organization chart provided by Defendants); and (2) the Search Terms agreed on by Defendants for Plaintiffs' Request for Production.

FACTUAL BACKGROUND AND SUMMARY OF CASE

A. Polly's Performance and Background at Corporate Company
B. Polly's Performance and Interactions with Darren
C. Polly's Complaints
D. Polly's Termination

CAUSES OF ACTION ALLEGED

Plaintiffs have alleged claims for:

CODING DEFENDANTS' DOCUMENTS

The purpose of this section is to provide you with guidance in issue spotting and coding in your review of our clients' documents. You will be coding for responsiveness, confidentiality, issues, and privilege.

1. **RESPONSIVENESS**
   a. **Withhold Privilege** – documents that fall within the Privilege Designation detailed below.
   b. **Needs Further Review** – any documents you may have a question on; please try to email the question first so as to not overuse this designation.
   c. **Technical Issue** – documents with a technical issue.
   d. **Nonresponsive** – Documents that do not fall within one of the below categories.
   e. **Responsive Documents** – those documents that fall within one of the categories:
      i. Here, list the categories of documents that you will be producing pursuant to the RFPs, keeping in mind any objections to these requests.
2. **ISSUE TAGS** – Use these tags for the review of both the inbound and client documents you will be reviewing. If you believe another issue tag would be helpful, do not hesitate to suggest it!
   a. Here, list tags for documents that will help you easily organize the information to documents that either support or negate various claims and defenses.
3. **PRIVILEGE** – the idea of privilege is complicated in this manner because there are involved attorneys who wear different hats and are parties to the litigation. If you determine a document should be withheld for privilege, mark the document as Withhold-Privilege along with a corresponding privilege designation – either Attorney Client Communication or Attorney Work Product.
   a. In determining whether a document is privileged you should keep in mind the following non-exhaustive list of attorneys/paralegals/law firms/legal domain names. If you come across any others, please email it to us:
      i. Here, list the names of law firms and attorneys known in the matter
4. **CONFIDENTIALITY** – the parties have entered into a protective order in this matter. Documents may require the following designation:
   a. Here, list the various confidentiality designations and when each should be applied.

<u>CODING PLAINTIFF'S INBOUND DOCUMENTS</u>

The purpose of this section is to provide you with guidance in issue spotting and coding in your review of inbound documents. You will be coding for issues only. Please refer to the issue list above.

Glossary

A

Acceptable encryption and key management policy – a policy that defines the standards for encrypting and managing sensitive data.

Acceptable use policy – a policy that is an agreement between a company and its employees expressing an intent to adhere to certain standards regarding usage of company hardware and software.

Access control policy – a policy that details requirements that specify how data can be accessed and who can access it.

Alpha-numeric identifier – unique identifier that contains letters and numbers combined.

Application software programs – program with specific uses, such as processing text, calculating numbers, sending e-mail, text and instant messaging, organizing large amounts of data, etc. Application software includes word processors, spreadsheets, email, text or instant messaging software, database managers, graphics, money managers, and games. These application programs generate electronic information that is then saved in proprietary computer files, which are referred to as native files.

Archival systems – long-term storage systems that host data that is no longer active.

Archiving and deletion policy – a policy that addresses archiving information, i.e., shifting infrequently accessed data to low-cost storage repositories, and ultimately deleting the data once a minimum retainment period has been reached.

Attorney-client privilege – under federal common law, the attorney-client privilege protects from disclosure any communications that involve only: clients, their counsel, and/or certain third parties, such as client-agents and attorney-agents, who may be involved without rendering the communication non-confidential. The communications must be confidential when they occur and are intended to be kept confidential, and they must be made for the purpose of obtaining or rendering legal advice.

B

Backup – a duplicate storage copy of a computer program, disc, or data. It is made for archiving purposes or for safeguarding valuable files from loss should the active copy be damaged or destroyed.

BSA – the Bank Secrecy Act; a law under which financial institutions are required to retain records for five years.

Bates numbering – a method of sequentially numbering pages with a reference number.

Boolean searches – an advanced method of keyword searching that permits word and phrase combinations using operators such AND, OR, NOT to limit or broaden searches. These are the same searches often used with Westlaw or LexisNexis.

Bring-your-own device policy (BYOD policy) – a set of rules that governs how employees utilize personal phones, laptops, and other devices for work.

C

CCPA – the California Consumer Privacy Act; a law that is aimed at giving consumers more control over the personal information that businesses collect about them. Under the CCPA, consumers have a right to know what type of personal information a business collects about them, how it is shared, how it can be deleted, and how to opt-out of the sharing of information.

Categorical privilege log – a privilege log that contains information in specific categories, rather than individual documents.

Categorization – a process where the reviewer creates a set of example documents that analytics uses as the basis for identifying and grouping other conceptually similar documents.

Clean desk policy – a policy that requires employees to keep their workspaces free of confidential or sensitive information, including client files and folders and external drives containing sensitive data.

Cleansing – removal of data from a file.

Cloud-based storage – an internet-based storage platform. Information is essentially housed on the cloud. Examples include OneDrive and SharePoint.

Clustering – a type of analytics that is designed to help organize data by grouping conceptually related documents by looking at ideas and similar text patterns.

Compression – the saving of a file in a reduced file size using a container file so that it can be smaller for purposes of easier transport among devices. It also often includes encryption of files.

Computer links/local area networks (LANs) – the means by which computers exchange data and talk to each other. LANS allow linked computers to share data, programs, storage, and printers. A server on a local area network (LAN) is a computer (or computers) that controls access to the network and its resources (such as hard drives, e-mail, text and instant messaging and printers). Information on servers is generally stored on hard drives or optical disks. Depending on the type of server, they are often the targets of discovery requests because of the ESI stored on them.

Concept search – a search that expands the search beyond the keywords chosen and returns documents relevant to the concept underlying the search terms.

Container file – a single file that contains one or more other files such as ZIP and PST files.

Coverage review – a type of Continuous Active Learning that serves up relevant and non-relevant documents to the reviewers. It is meant to quickly separate documents into responsive and non-responsive documents so that productions can be made as quickly as possible.

Custodial de-duplication – this process compares an incoming document against documents already in a review platform for a given custodian. This method will leave copies in each custodian's processed mailbox but not leave multiple copies in each custodian's mailbox.

Custodian – a person who owns data.

D

Data breach response policy – a policy that defines the procedures for dealing with a data breach within an organization.

De-duplication – the process of removing secondary copies of a document so that only one copy remains.

De-NISTing – the method of reducing the number of documents subject to review by removing file types that are unlikely to be responsive or have evidentiary value. Examples of file types removed during de-NISTing are files used to execute computer programs, help files, and font files. Many e-discovery review platforms offer the ability to de-NIST, and application of this process is commonplace.

Device management policies – a policy that establishes rules for how a company-owned device is used and secured. These policies may address rules against sharing devices with non-employees.

Disaster recovery plan policy – a policy that details a company's strategy for handling unplanned events such as natural disasters, cyberattacks, or other data-damaging occurrences.

Doc ID – a document identifier that is a unique name for each file in the system.

E

Electronic Discovery Reference Model (EDRM) – the standard by which litigators and litigation technologists provide an e-discovery roadmap; it is an atlas to managing and minimizing the issues that arise when electronically stored information is identified, preserved, collected, processed, reviewed/analyzed, and produced.

Email (cloud based) – a method of email delivery and storage hosted and maintained by an outside provider. Information is essentially housed on the cloud. Examples include Microsoft Outlook, Yahoo Mail, Google Gmail, and Mozilla Thunderbird.

Email (server based) – also called a mail server, essentially a computer system that sends and receives emails. The information is essentially housed internally. Examples include Amazon SES, Halton MTA, Microsoft Exchange Server, and OpenSMTPD.

Email thread – a series of related emails that are organized and linked together to form a conversation. The first message is usually at the bottom, while the most recent message is seen first at the top.

Encrypted hard drive or thumb/USB drive – drive encryption is a technology that places data on hard drive or thumb drive so that the data cannot be read by anyone who does not have access to the appropriate key or password.

Enterprise applications – a large software system platform designed to operate in a corporate environment.

Enterprise data – data shared by the users of an organization, generally across departments or regions.

ESI – information created, manipulated, communicated, stored, and best utilized in digital form, requiring the use of computer hardware and software.

ESI Protocol – a negotiated document that expressly states how the parties to a litigation should produce ESI, and ideally, this will be drafted and negotiated once the attorney has more information on the amount, types, and location of her client's data.

F

Fact work product – protects from disclosure documents and tangible things that are prepared both in anticipation of litigation, and by or for a party; a party's representative (such as counsel, agent, consultant, retained expert, or employer); or counsel's representative (such as an agent, consultant, or retained expert).

FERPA – the Family Education Rights and Privacy Act; a law that protects the privacy of student education records and gives parents certain rights with respect to these records prior to a student reaching the age of 18. Parents or eligible students have the right to inspect and review the student's education records and to request corrections to the records. Under FERPA, institutions are required to retain data during a student's active attendance plus six years after they are no longer active.

File system – the area of the computer system that provides organization and storage of information and programmatic functions.

Fuzzy search – a search function available in many review platforms that finds words based on spelling similarities.

G

Global de-duplication – this process compares an incoming document against all other documents in a review workspace.

GLBA – the Gramm-Leach-Bliley Act; this law requires financial institutions to explain their information-sharing practices to their customers and to safeguard sensitive data, including setting specified retention and destruction periods.

H

Hash values – unique algorithm generated identifiers based on file information for the purpose of creating an identifier used for duplicate identification.

HIPAA – the Health Insurance Portability and Accountability Act of 1996; a federal law that protects sensitive patient health information by regulating the use and disclosure of an individual's health information by covered entities, such as healthcare providers and insurance companies. The Privacy Rule portion of HIPAA ensures that individuals understand and control how their information is being used. The Security Rule portion of HIPAA protects all individually identifiable health information a covered entity creates, receives, maintains, or transmits in electronic form by creating standards under which patient data is safeguarded.

I

Information governance – the policies, processes and procedures involved in using and managing business information in order to drive maximum value, while minimizing information-related risk.

Information security policy – rules and guidelines that a company implements to protect its information systems and to ultimately keep its data secure. These policies ultimately govern security surrounding the access and use of information.

IT infrastructure – a method of organizing the computer system and network management of an organization. It will generally reflect the organization's work processes integrated with the computer network.

K

Keyword – search terms are input into a search function and a list of documents searched containing a search term is returned.

L

Legacy data – electronic information that has been used in prior software and hardware configurations.

Legal holds – communications sent to individuals with potentially relevant information, placing these individuals on notice to cease any deletion or destruction of relevant material, whether automatic or manual.

Legal right standard – the legal right to control or obtain the documents upon demand.

Legal right plus notification standard – states that parties must not only have the legal right to obtain the information but also must notify the opposing party about potentially relevant information held by third parties.

Linear review – method of review whereby attorney reviews all documents without the application of search terms or analytics to cull the document population down.

Loose file – a standalone file not part of something else such as a group of files or attached to an email.

M

MD5 hash – an algorithm used to calculate a hash value.

Metadata – a set of data that describes and gives information about other data.

Metadata only privilege log – a log that contains an export of agreed-upon metadata fields without the need to enter in separate privilege descriptions for each entry.

Mobile devices – cell phones, including instant and text messaging applications, email applications, third-party communication applications.

N

Near dupes analytics – a type of analytics that looks at the largest document and determines how similar the near dupes must be to qualify as a dupe.

Network – a central linked group of computers.

Network servers – a computer program or device that manages network resources and receives and answers requests from clients. The information is essentially housed internally.

Normalization – equalization across a dataset to make all things consistent.

O

OCR – sometimes referred to as text recognition, an OCR program extracts and repurposes data from scanned documents, camera images, and image-only PDFs. OCR software singles out letters on the image, puts them into words, and then puts the words into sentences, thus enabling access to and editing of the original content.

Opinion work product – protects from disclosure documents and tangible things that are prepared in anticipation of litigation and by a party's counsel or other representative. This work product includes or reflects the creator's mental impressions, conclusions, opinions, and legal theories.

P

Password policy – details the requirements of passwords to access company data, including password length and inclusion of special characters. This policy may also detail how often passwords must be changed and include best practices for keeping passwords safe and secure.

PCI DSS – the Payment Card Industry Data Security Standard; a set of data retention policies and procedures that ensures the security of credit, debit, and cash card transactions and protects cardholders against misuse of their personal information.

Personnel security policy – a policy for hiring, training, and monitoring employees who have access to sensitive data.

Phonic searches – a search that provides results that sound alike.

Practical ability standard – requires a party to preserve, collect, search, and produce documents and ESI irrespective of that party's legal entitlement or actual physical possession of the documents if a party has the practical ability.

Prioritized review – a type of Continuous Active Learning tool that serves up the most relevant documents to the reviewers until almost no relevant documents are left.

Processing – the intake of file information and links to files for use in a database that provides a collaboration environment.

PST files – a file format used to store items like calendar events, contacts, and email messages.

R

Records management policy – focus on a company's procedures for managing its records. These policies address how records are created, stored, accessed, and ultimately destroyed or archived.

Remote working policy – or work-from-home policy, is a set of guidelines that outlines how and when it's appropriate for employees to work outside the office.

Retention and disposal schedules – a policy that details the types of records held within a company, the minimum period such records should be retained, and the actions taken once that minimum period has been reached.

Rule 26(f) Conference – a conference that must take place at least 21 days before a scheduling conference is to be held so that parties may confer about a discovery plan.

Rule 502(d) Order – FRE 502 permits a federal court to enter an order stating that production of documents protected by the attorney-client privilege or work product doctrine does not waive those protections in the specific litigation or any other federal or state proceeding.

S

Secure FTP (SFTP or secure file transfer protocol) – a file transfer protocol that uses specific encryption to transfer files between systems securely. Many organizations have an SFTP already set up through which data can be shared and received.

Shared drives – shared spaces where teams can easily store, search, and access their files anywhere, from any device.

Social media (Instagram, X (formerly known as Twitter), TikTok) – a tool by which we facilitate the sharing of ideas and information through virtual networks. This category of data is constantly evolving with the development of new social media platforms, and collection methods for the various types of social media will vary.

Stemming search – a search that returns all variations of a root word.

Storage media – used to store data from an electronic device. Many devices today have capabilities for both fixed (internal) storage/memory and the ability to store data simultaneously to removable storage media (including online, cloud internet sites).

Structured database (on prem and/or cloud) – typically categorized as quantitative data, structured data is highly organized data that is decipherable by proprietary software. Information for structured databases can be hosted internally on a server or remotely in the cloud. Examples include SQL databases and POS data.

Synonym search – a search that uses a thesaurus and returns documents containing either the search term or a synonym.

System software – controls and coordinates the operation of the various types of equipment and operating system in a computer. The most important type of system software is a set of programs called the operating system. The operating system controls the activity of a computer whether it is a desktop, laptop, PDA, or other type of computing device.

T

Technology-assisted review (TAR) – uses a series of algorithms to quickly sort through the documents to make determinations as to responsiveness, hotness, and other categories. Subject matter experts on the case team essentially create a training set of documents that can be coded for relevance, specific issues, and privilege. The computer then uses algorithms to apply the same coding decisions to the remaining documents.

Third party collaboration applications (Slack, Microsoft Teams, Google Workspace) – communication platforms and collaboration hubs that includes instant messaging, voice and video calls, and tools to help groups share information and work together.

Third party messaging applications (WhatsApp, Facebook Messenger) – an application other than text messaging that allows individuals to message each other.

Tiffing – slang term to mean the creation of a tiff image file from a native version of the file.

TIFFs – a file format that is a static image of a file.

U

Unitization – the process of packaging documents into their logical family.

Unprocessable – files that cannot be opened or read for extracting the metadata and inserting into a database.

Unstructured data – information that is not arranged according to a preset data model and therefore cannot be stored in a traditional database.

W

Work product doctrine – protects documents and tangible things that are prepared in anticipation of litigation by (or for) another party or its representative from disclosure to third parties.

Z

Zip file – a computer file whose contents of one or more files are compressed for storage or transmission. Essentially, zip files take large files and compress their contents so they take up less space.

Index